Comfort
in Uncertain Times

15 The Chambers, Vineyard
Abingdon OX14 3FE
brf.org.uk

Bible Reading Fellowship is a charity (233280)
and company limited by guarantee (301324),
registered in England and Wales

ISBN 978 0 85746 628 0
First published 2022
10 9 8 7 6 5 4 3 2 1 0
All rights reserved

Text by Rachel Turner 2022
This edition © Bible Reading Fellowship 2022
Cover artwork © Rebecca J Hall

The author asserts the moral right to be identified as the author of this work

Acknowledgements
Unless otherwise stated, scripture quotations are taken from Easy-to-Read
Version, copyright © 2006 by Bible League international.

Scripture quotations marked NLT are taken from The Holy Bible, New Living
Translation, copyright © 1996, 2004, 2007, 2013. Used by permission of Tyndale
House Publishers, Inc., Carol Stream, Illinois 60188. All rights reserved.

Every effort has been made to trace and contact copyright owners for material
used in this resource. We apologise for any inadvertent omissions or errors, and
would ask those concerned to contact us so that full acknowledgement can be
made in the future.

A catalogue record for this book is available from the British Library

Printed and bound by CPI Group (UK) Ltd, Croydon CR0 4YY

Comfort in Uncertain Times

HELPING CHILDREN DRAW CLOSE TO GOD THROUGH BIBLICAL STORIES OF ANXIETY, LOSS AND TRANSITION

RACHEL TURNER

For my godchildren –
Eli, Zeke, Tabby, Emily and Caitlin.

May your uncertain times be filled with
God's comfort and joy.

Acknowledgements

To Caleb Turner: we have walked through so many uncertain times together, and it has been one of my greatest joys to learn about who God is with you. Thank you for praying for me, giving me your wisdom and advice, and for letting me play with you.

To my husband, Mark Turner: no book gets made without you. Thank you for enduring my cyclical rants and wanderings and always helping me land well.

To my mother, Susan Hart: thank you for being my mother through every phase of my life. I need you in different ways, but I always need you. Thank you for teaching me and growing me.

To my father, Terry Hart: thank you for holding me up in your prayers, and equipping me for life constantly.

To Becky Sedgwick and Anna Hawken: you daily teach me what it truly means to be part of a team who loves each other well, and delights in both weaknesses and strengths. You are the sisters of my heart. I cannot do what I do without you.

To the BRF team: thank you for your faithfulness and relentless grace.

To all my friends who answer late night WhatsApp messages for prayer and read drafts with brutal honesty and love, Ell and Jo Ireton, James and Susie Yeates, Elle Bird, Sarah Hogben, Rhi O'Rourke and Elaine Webster: thank you for your tolerance and grace.

Acknowledgements

Contents

INTRODUCTION 9

1   IN THE BEGINNING...15

2   PRISCILLA AND AQUILA.................................19

3   A SHEPHERD'S TALE 25

4   SHEM AND THE LONG WAIT..........................35

5   PRESSURE IN PHILIPPI 41

6   THE FIVE SISTERS AND THE UNFAIR LAW 49

7   SINGING IN A CAVE......................................57

8   THE FOURTH MAN...63

9   MARTHA AND THE BAD DAY.........................73

10 THE DESK OF THE KING...............................81

11 DAVID AND THE DECISION 89

12 NO WORDS..97

13 THE RISK 103

14 THE SHORT WAY HOME..............................111

15 UNTIL WE MEET AGAIN..............................119

Introduction

Life is full of uncertainty. From friendships changing to moving house, the loss of a family member or the anxiety and worry of a world that never stays the same. All of our children will face uncertainty, both now and in the future.

Uncertainty is hard. Our children can struggle to cope with change, crushing grief or cycles of anxiety. Some children feel a deep sense of unease or don't know how to talk about or process their experiences.

Everything inside us as adults wants to make it better for them, to smooth the path and fix what is causing them such turmoil. But most of the time, that isn't possible. The circumstances are still there the next day and the day after.

The joy of the Christian faith is that our children can learn to walk with God in these uncertain seasons. All of God's promises are for our children right now, and they need his guidance, comfort, peace and courage. In uncertain times, we can help them connect with the God who is powerful, who loves them and is with them whatever they're going through.

God never said that we would have an easy, uncomplicated, pain-free life when we become Christians. His plan is better than that. He desires that we have life to the full (John 10:10), be transformed to be more like Jesus (2 Corinthians 3:18) and become daily aware of the depth of his love and our purpose with him (Ephesians 3:18).

The question is not *if* the storms of life come but *when*. There were two times when the disciples encountered Jesus in choppy waters with powerful winds. One time, Jesus calmed the storm. The other time, he walked on water and invited Peter to step out of the boat on to the lake while the winds continued to blow and the waves continued to rise. On both occasions, he showed his disciples who he is and what he can do in a storm.

Our children may be facing uncertainty. The most important gift we can give is to show them who God is and what he is doing in the midst of it. We can empower them to walk through the storms with a faithful God who is just as powerful in uncertainty as he is in the calm. We can help them hold fast to the God who weaves all things together for good and is faithful to guide and comfort. We can connect them to the God who hears them and responds, who provides and rescues, and who gives them peace and purpose when they feel helpless.

Every person's circumstances of uncertainty are different. This book can never address all the specific situations you may find yourselves in. I hope, rather, that this book will give you and your children the tools and conversations to find God in the midst of your journey and learn to walk with him in it, shifting our eyes from the winds and the waves of what surrounds us to the one who walks it with us.

This book will help you as a family gather and explore the tools and theology of who God is and what he does when we are in transition, anxiety or loss. It will help you coach your children to have long-term strategies and foundations to weather a lifetime of change and uncertainty.

Making this book work for your family

Within this book are 15 stories, each followed by some conversation starters and suggestions for ways to connect with God. Each story will help you jump into an aspect of who God is in anxiety, loss or transition. Each has one key truth to explore together about what God is doing in our circumstances. Some will give you tools to pray, to see things differently or to open up conversations about feelings and faith.

Each story starts with a summary of the key truth and idea of the story, for you as a parent to be able to see and feel comfortable with where the chapter is headed. After that you will find the story, conversation starters and ways to connect with God about what is coming up in our hearts and lives.

Reading the stories provides a foundation to begin a discussion. The stories are intended as a jumping-off point for you to continue the conversation, ask questions, share with each other and connect with God about whatever you are facing. The real equipping happens in the room between your family and God.

The key truths are what we want to embed into our children's hearts, and people choose to do that in various ways. Some families like sticking to the book's ideas of discussing and praying, while other families enjoy doing something tangible afterwards while they talk and pray to build a memory of the key truths. Some draw pictures of the truths, write them on posters to put on the wall or make a memory journal. How you explore these ideas is entirely up to you.

All the stories build an understanding of who God is in uncertainty, and I recommend you read them all to build a robust and broad foundation of truth in your children's lives for all the circumstances they may face.

A note for you

1 It's okay to feel what you feel. When children struggle with anxiety, change, grief or uncertainty, the whole family often experience the same situation. You yourself may be in deep pain or worry. It is okay to feel those things and still help your child in it. You do not have to be in a perfect emotional place to help your child. This whole book is an opportunity to journey alongside each other and with God through a storm. One of the greatest gifts we can give our children is a close-up experience of an imperfect person finding their way with God in difficulty. While we do not want to dump all our raw emotions on to our children, it can be helpful for them to get glimpses of how God helps you in those emotions. There are questions to discuss with your children in each chapter. Please be open and honest, letting your children see a bit of your faith journey by answering those questions yourself, too. Share your stories, talk about your wonderings. Don't worry about getting answers right. Free yourself to authentically explore the ideas and experiences with your children. It will significantly help your children to know that walking through uncertainty with God is a process that even adults are still learning. If you or your children struggle to tell stories, we have included links to videos so that you can listen to normal people telling their God-stories of life in uncertainty. See **parentingforfaith.org/comfort-stories**.

2 Conversation and prayer are essential parts of this exploration. It can be tempting to simply read the stories and skip the rest, but the equipping and progress happen in the conversations and God-connections. Pick a time to explore this book when it works for you. There is no right time or perfect method. Some people may choose breakfast, or before dinner, bedtime or the weekends.

Some may read the story at night and discuss it the next day, or some may have it be something to explore together at a lunch picnic on a Saturday. However you do it, feel free to make it your own. You know your family best; you are the expert in how your children think and feel. Please do this in whatever way you feel will work best for them, knowing that adjustment may be needed as you go!

3   Helping children to connect with God in their own way through prayer is an important part of supporting their faith journey. At Parenting for Faith, we call it 'Chat and Catch', enabling children to chat to God authentically and tune into his communications back to them. To explore these ideas further, see **parentingforfaith.org/chat-and-catch** or the Parenting for Faith free online course for deeper teaching and ideas at **parentingforfaith.org/course**.

4   In the prayer or conversation times, I often refer to the 'situation' your children are in. As you lead through conversations and prayers, please swap out that word for the actual situation they are experiencing. It will help make their engagement so much clearer and personal for your children if you say, 'Tell God how you feel about your worries' or 'Tell God how you feel about Grandma dying' rather than 'Tell God how you feel about your situation.'

5   I often also use the general term 'God' in many of the prayer times. Every family is different in how they like to address God. Some people like to pray primarily to the Lord, Father God, Jesus or Holy Spirit. Please pray however you feel comfortable.

6   Coaching our children through grief, anxiety and change is an ongoing process. It's like teaching someone how to swim. It is a skill that will last them a lifetime, but learning it takes practice, attempts and failures, and surprising successes. It grows little by little with experience. As you explore the tools and theology, how you apply them to circumstances as you go forward will continue to help your children today, next year and the year after. This

experience will be creating a toolbox for you to pull from for a lifetime of coaching your children.

7   God loves to meet with his children, and he wants them to know his peace in their uncertain times. He is faithful to be responding to them as they connect with him and as you talk through these situations. He promises so much to them, and as we help them see and connect with God in their uncertainty, they will know him more.

May God fill you with his peace and confidence as you boldly wade into this adventure with your children. May he give you courage and wisdom as you equip your children for a life with a good God in a stormy world.

1

In the beginning

Genesis 1

KEY TRUTH
God created a changing world.

Sometimes we feel that change is something to resist, but change is part of how God created us to grow, develop and discover new parts of him. Not all change is sent by God, but in all change God grows us and walks with us.

Story

In the beginning was God. Before there was anything, there was God. And he was the same as he is now: wonderful, kind, perfect, powerful, fair, loving and wise. And he was planning. Oh, the plans he was making! Oh, the wonders he was designing! They were beyond anything we could ever dream or imagine.

He waited until the perfect time. The time that was just right. And then… he spoke.

The word of God can make all things happen, and with a few words, he began his great creation. He could have decided to make his creation so that it would all stay still and perfect, like a beautiful painting. But God is much more creative than that. He wanted something better. God's creation grows and changes.

God designed the sun and moon so that the earth could change from day to night and back to day again.

God shaped the oceans to come in and flow out as the tides change. He made plants that grow from tiny seeds into trees so tall we can't even see the tops.

God made birds, animals and insects that grow from tiny eggs into full-grown beasts and then make their own new babies, in an endless cycle of life.

And God made us – you and me – to be a part of this ever-changing world. We, too, are growing. Our bodies get bigger, and our brains get wiser. We make mistakes, and we try new things. We change a little every day.

God made the world so that today is never the same as tomorrow. And when he looked at it all, he saw that it was good.

Good, because in the middle of change, he can show us who he is. In the middle of change, he can help us grow into who he has designed us to be. In the middle of change, he can walk side-by-side with us for all of our tomorrows.

And that is *very* good.

Conversation starters

Let's answer some questions together. I'll answer them too.

- What part of the story did you like or find interesting or surprising? Why?
- What does this story tell us about God?
- Why do you think God made a world that grows and changes rather than stays the same?
- Would you have made the same choice? Why or why not?
- Do you like when things change? Why or why not?

- Not all changes come from God, but he always grows us and walks with us when it happens. Are things changing now? How do you feel about it?
- What are some of the ways God has been growing us and walking with us now?

Connect with God

Let's connect with God and chat with him about this. I'll read some things for us to chat to God about, and then we can all chat to God either in our heads or whisper into our hands so no one else but God can hear *(if they are under 7)*.

- Tell God what you think is the best change that God created.
- Tell God how you feel when things change around you. *(You may want to list some changes that your child has recently experienced.)*
- Imagine a picture in your mind of you and God walking together, or feel free to draw one. God can see that picture. Tell God how that picture makes you feel.
- God, come close to us now and be next to us through the changes we are going through. Let's wait quietly for a few seconds as God comes close. *(Wait for ten seconds.)*
- *You may want to finish with a prayer* – Thank you, God, that you are so creative that you made a world that grows and changes, including us. Thank you for showing us who you are and being with us through every change that comes.

2

Priscilla and Aquila

Acts 18

> **KEY TRUTH**
> God weaves all things together for good.

An angry emperor forced Priscilla and Aquila to move out of their home and travel far away. They arrived in a new city without friends or a place to live. But God turned that unexpected sadness into a wonderful adventure for them. They led the first church in that city, and got to have Paul, the writer of lots of the Bible, live in their home. God turned something evil and horrible into good for so many people. God can weave anything into good for us and others.

Story

'Aquila, have you seen my purple scarf? I can't find it anywhere!' called Priscilla to her husband. She opened the lid of another bag to see if it was there, then shook her head. One of the worst parts of moving was looking for something you've already packed.

'No idea where it is!' Aquila called from the upstairs bedroom. 'Maybe it was loaded on to the ship with all the other boxes.'

'I just don't want to lose it. My dad gave it to me!' Priscilla closed the bag with a 'humph' and stood with her hands on her hips in frustration.

Their little house looked so empty now. This morning the ship's crew came and collected all their boxes and furniture for their trip to their new home across the sea.

Priscilla called again: 'Timothy will be here any minute to take us to the docks. We don't want to be late and miss the boat!'

Aquila came down, holding a little wooden toy. 'Look what we almost forgot!' he said, handing it to her. 'The little fish that our friend Chloe carved for us when she first started making toys.' They both smiled, and Priscilla ran her fingers over its bumps and grooves.

Priscilla sighed and looked around her. 'I loved all the good times we had in this house. Remember when we first met Chloe at the market stall? She had so many angry ideas about God. But we kept inviting her for dinner, and sharing our experiences about Jesus, and right *here* she talked to him in prayer for the first time.' Priscilla smiled at the empty corner in the room.

'We have so many memories of what God did in people's lives in this house, week after week. I'll miss leading our little church. Eating together, reading scriptures, and laughing and praying together. I loved every minute.'

Priscilla looked over the room one last time and sighed. Then she heard a sharp knock at the door. With a heavy heart, she opened it, and there was Timothy grinning. His young face was lit up with excitement, and his arms were loaded with bulging bags. 'Are you ready? I'm so excited. This is going to be a great adventure!'

Priscilla smiled weakly, 'Well, I can't say I'm excited yet.' A wave of sadness washed over her as they walked out and closed their front door for the last time. Priscilla patted her husband's back, and they began walking down the road towards the dock.

Timothy seemed to be buzzing with excitement. 'I love travelling with Paul and telling people about Jesus. I can't wait to see what Ephesus is going to be like. Have you ever been there? I've never been there. Did you know they have a huge temple there with a massive statue in it? It's famous!' Timothy chattered on as he walked alongside them.

When they entered the marketplace, Aquila's face lit up. He took off, weaving in and out of the stalls, saying goodbye to the shopkeepers he knew, hugging friends and laughing with people one last time. Priscilla waved to them from a distance and smiled, and they called out encouragements to come back and visit. She promised they would. Aquila emerged from the end of the marketplace with a basket full of last-minute gifts from their shopkeeper friends.

Aquila hooked Priscilla's arm with his arm, and nudged the basket towards her. 'Would you like an orange? Selina sends her love.' Tears sprung to Aquila's eyes. 'I will miss everybody so much. We have made such good friends here. People who love us and make us laugh. My heart hurts just thinking about it.'

Timothy smiled at Aquila. 'Have you always lived here? You seem to know everybody.'

Aquila shook his head. 'No, actually we used to live in Rome. Our whole family lived there. I was born there, and I met and married Priscilla there. We loved it in Rome.'

'If you liked it so much in Rome, why did you leave?' Timothy asked.

Aquila shrugged his shoulders. 'The emperor Claudius forced the Jews to leave Rome. He didn't want us there. We didn't have a choice. We had to leave or be killed.'

Timothy paused for a moment. 'That must have been awful.'

Priscilla nodded. 'It was. We thought our whole life was destroyed. We didn't know where to go. We trusted God to lead us to wherever he wanted us, and we ended up here. God didn't speak to us or tell us with a big voice, "Go here." We just felt really peaceful when our boat landed here, and we felt that it was right to stay.' The road turned, and then they skipped down a series of stairs. Several seagulls squawked overhead as they neared the docks.

'A few weeks after we moved here, Paul showed up,' said Aquila, shifting his basket. 'We heard him telling people about Jesus, and we wanted to help. It just so happened that he was a tentmaker, like us, and he needed a place to stay, so we asked him to stay with us.'

The docks came into sight at the end of the road. Large and small boats were bobbing in the water and gently swaying in the breeze. Priscilla took a deep breath. 'When we were on the ship from Rome, not knowing where we were going, I never could have imagined what God would do with our lives. He turned the worst experience of our lives into the most wonderful place of love and adventure. Here, God gave us purpose and friends and opportunities to see him work. And now he's asking us to leave.'

'Well, I'm so glad you're coming with us,' said Timothy. He smiled. 'Hey, look, there's Paul!' In the distance, the tiny figure of Paul stood in front of a large wooden boat with tall masts and bright white sails. Paul was waving enthusiastically. Timothy waved back and started sprinting towards him.

Priscilla stood still and reached her hand out to Aquila. They turned to look back at the city they had loved. This time, rather than sadness, she felt grateful. She whispered, 'Thank you, God, for the gift of this place to live. I trust you, God. I don't know what this new place will bring, but I know you will be there, and you'll have more love and adventures for us. Thank you.'

Aquila squeezed her hand. 'Ready?'

Priscilla turned around towards the boat and waved at Paul. 'Yes, I am.'

Conversation starters

Let's answer some questions together. I'll answer them too.

- What part of the story did you like or find interesting or surprising? Why?
- What does this story tell us about God?
- When change happens, it can sometimes feel like it is very bad. Priscilla and Aquila had to move away from their home and didn't want to. Have you ever felt like a bad change was happening to you? What did it feel like?
- The Bible says that God can work all things together for the good of those who love him (Romans 8:28). Can you tell a story of a time when God's good came out of a tough situation? I'll start. *(Or use a story at parentingforfaith.org/comfort-stories.)*

Connect with God

Let's connect with God and chat with him about this.

- God, it's sometimes hard to see what good can come out of… *(fill in the circumstances your child or family is experiencing)*, but we know you will do it.
- Let's tell God times that we know he has brought good out of hard things from our life, other's stories or the Bible.
- *Grab some drawing paper and colouring pens and have everybody draw a picture of a hard situation they are in, whether it is a general sense of anxiety or a situation of change or grief.*
- *Add God to the picture, working or weaving things together for good. What might he be doing? Where is he?*
- *You may want to finish with a prayer* – Thank you, God, that you are a perfect weaver of our lives, and no bad thing is too big for you. You bring good into our todays and tomorrows. We look forward to what you will do with the situation we are in.
- *Chat about your pictures with each other.*

3
A shepherd's tale

Psalm 23; Matthew 18:10-14

KEY TRUTH

God is like a good shepherd, guiding and comforting us.

Jesus describes himself as a good shepherd who goes ahead of us, guides us with his voice and finds us when we are lost. In uncertainty, we may not know what is next, but we can trust that we are not alone and that God himself will guide us through. We all need a good shepherd, especially in a time of uncertainty.

Story

Caleb strode the final steps to the top of the hill and looked around intently. He flung his arms in the air in frustration. 'Grandad,' he called down. 'You were right. We *are* missing a lamb! I can't see it anywhere!'

The evening sun made long dark shadows against the rocks and boulders. The lamb could be hiding or stuck between any of them, and he'd never see it.

Caleb looked down and saw his grandad walking slowly up to him. Farther down the hill, he could see his sister, Anna, weaving around the sheep scattered on the hillside and playing with a few of the more excited lambs. Caleb had been so excited when his mum told him that they were going to go visit his grandad for the week. His grandad owned hundreds of sheep, and this year Grandad had promised to take Caleb and Anna out to the fields to learn what it was like to be a shepherd. It sounded like such a great adventure, but after half a day with the sheep, Caleb wasn't so sure anymore. Shepherding wasn't what he thought it would be. And now it appeared that they had lost a lamb.

Grandad was almost at the top of the hill. He used his big stick with a hook on the end as a brace to help him walk up the last bits, sticking it hard into the ground to steady himself with every step. His dark skin was wrinkled with a lifetime of sun and work, and his short beard was specked with grey and white streaks. He was breathing hard from the climb as he said, 'Sheep don't really have a great sense of direction, which is why they need a shepherd to guide them. Without a shepherd they can get into all kinds of danger. Sometimes they wander off, and it's our job to go find them.' He looked around at the rock-filled land. 'Hmm. If I were a sheep, where would I go?'

As they searched around, Caleb heard his sister shout up, 'It's getting dark! Are we going home now?'

Grandad smiled at Caleb and called back, 'No, we aren't! Tomorrow we're taking the sheep to a new pasture, so we will camp here and watch over them tonight. We need to keep them safe and make sure no wolves come and hurt them or take the lambs.'

'Woo hoo!' Anna shouted, and started running towards them. 'We get to sleep out here with the sheep and fight wolves? That's so great!'

Grandad chuckled. 'I've seen how good you are with your slingshot. Maybe you'll get a chance to use it tonight.'

'Eeee!' Anna squealed in excitement.

Caleb's stomach churned. A whole night outside with the wolves didn't seem like the best idea.

Grandad slapped his thighs. 'Right, well, we need to get ready for the evening. Anna, could you please start making a fire for us? I'll leave my big bag here. You'll notice some extra blankets in there for tonight.

Caleb and I will go round up the sheep. Please keep an eye out for our lost one.'

Grandad and Caleb headed down the hill towards the sheep. They were spread out like enormous white leaves all over the hillside. Caleb ran ahead trying to get the sheep to go towards his grandad. Every time he got close to them, they would jump in surprise and then run away in all sorts of directions. 'Grandad, what am I doing wrong?' He rubbed his head in frustration.

Grandad patted him on the shoulder. 'It was an excellent effort, but they don't recognise you yet.' He turned to the field and said, 'Come on sheep, come with me!', and then he started walking back towards the hill. The sheep near Grandad began to follow him. Caleb was astonished. His grandad kept singing and calling to them, and slowly they all began to follow along towards the base of the hill.

Caleb walked alongside his grandad. 'How do you get them to follow you?'

Grandad laughed. 'They recognise my voice. Sheep are comforted by the voice of the shepherd. It makes them feel safe. When they follow my voice, they know they'll always find food and water and shelter and protection. I know where the water is in the desert. They don't. I know where the good food is. They don't. I know where the dangers are that they can't see. They don't. They just know that when they are with me, I'll make sure they get what they need.'

As sunset turned into night, his grandad stood near the little stream at the base of the hill, still chatting to the sheep and singing occasionally. The sheep began to clump together, chewing the grass and drinking from the stream. Slowly they began to lay down and rest. They looked so content.

Caleb frowned. 'If sheep follow your voice, how do they get lost?'

Grandad laughed. 'Some are just stubborn and want to go their own way. Some forget to pay attention to my voice and just wander away and can't find their way back. It doesn't matter why they wander off. It just matters that they are mine and that I will find them, no matter how lost they are.' He looked out over the flock.

It looked nice to be a sheep – if you had a good shepherd like his grandad.

The stars had come out and the fields were dark. The moon shone brightly, lighting all the fields with a blue glow.

Anna called down, 'Are you coming up to the fire? I found food in Grandad's bag!'

Grandad laughed. 'Well, of course there is food. I'm not going to let my assistant shepherds starve! I'll be up soon. I still have one sheep out here that isn't with my flock. I need to go look for him. Anna, you look after these sheep while I go look for the others.'

Anna leapt to her feet. 'Yes! I'll get my slingshot ready. Come on, wolves!'

Caleb gazed up at the fire and food. He was hungry, but he also really wanted to find this little lamb. 'I'll come with you, Grandad.'

They headed off into the dark, the fire flickering on the small hill behind them. Caleb reviewed in his mind all the places they had walked earlier that day, while his grandad called out with the hope his sheep would hear him and come. Caleb remembered a small bunch of bushes near some rocks that had snagged his clothes that morning. Maybe a small sheep could have gotten stuck there too?

'Grandad, I have an idea,' he said, then sped ahead and retraced their journey. In the moonlight, he saw the small outcrop of rocks with the spiky bush. And something in there was rustling. 'There, Grandad!

There!' Caleb began to run towards the bush, and then he saw the tiny lamb trapped in the branches. 'We found her! We found her!' he yelled.

The lamb was weak, and her little cries could barely be heard. Grandad handed Caleb his long shepherd's crook. Caleb carefully pushed aside the branches with it, and then he used the hook to pull the lamb out of the thick bush. She baaed softly, and Caleb picked her up and held her to his chest. He could feel her little heart thumping against his fingers. She nestled into his arms, shivering slightly.

Grandad smiled. 'Well done! That was some excellent shepherding right there.'

Caleb felt so protective over this little lost lamb. He held her in his arms during the long walk back through the thin moonlight and towards the flickering campfire in the distance. He petted her head and talked to her gently about how brave she was and how she was safe now.

As they neared the flock at the bottom of the hill, a high-pitched whistle sounded out. Caleb was puzzled and then a small rock landed hard at his feet.

'Stay away from my sheep, you wolves!' Anna yelled from the darkness.

'It's us! It's us!' Grandad laughed.

'Sorry! Hi Grandad,' Anna crowed.

As Caleb approached the flock, a mamma sheep began to trot towards him, bleating with joy. The little lamb in his arms wiggled to get free, and Caleb put it down. The mamma sheep nestled the lamb, and began to feed her. Caleb felt so proud, seeing all the sheep together and safe.

'Let's get some food, Caleb,' Grandad said.

Caleb smiled. 'Good night, little one,' he said to the lamb.

He turned and started walking up the hill. Then he heard tiny footsteps and looked down to see the little lamb at his feet.

Grandad smiled. 'Looks like this one recognises *your* voice now. Sometimes one sheep needs a bit more comfort than others. Bring her up with us.'

Caleb felt so happy he thought his heart might burst. He scooped up the lamb into his arms again, saying, 'You gotta stay close to your shepherd. No wandering off!'

As they all sat together around the fire, Grandad spoke quietly. 'King David was a shepherd, too, several thousands of years ago. He often spent nights on the hills with God, watching his sheep. I'd like you to listen to his words and tell me what you think.'

The fire crackled, and the little lamb shifted around in Caleb's arms.

Grandad's deep voice rumbled pleasantly as he spoke. 'The Lord is my shepherd; I have all that I need. He lets me rest in green meadows; he leads me beside peaceful streams. He renews my strength. He guides me along right paths, bringing honour to his name. Even when I walk through the darkest valley, I will not be afraid, for you are close beside me. Your rod and your staff protect and comfort me.'*

Caleb and his family sat in silence, the cool breeze bringing to them the quiet sounds of the resting flock. If Grandad was a *good* shepherd, then God must be the best one ever.

God, Caleb said in his heart, *I am so glad I get to be one of your sheep.*

---

* Psalm 23:1–4 (NLT)

Caleb smiled at the flock and continued: *God, you are my shepherd. I really need one. Help me know your voice. Guide me where to go. Keep me safe and close to you.*

Caleb looked down, feeling the delicate warmth of the sleeping lamb in his arms.

Come find me when I feel lost, and hold me like this when I need to feel safe.

Caleb looked at his Grandad. This really did turn out to be a great day after all.

Conversation starters

Let's answer some questions together. I'll answer them too.

- What part of the story did you like or find interesting or surprising? Why?
- What does this story tell us about God?
- God says he is our good shepherd, with us being like his little sheep. How is he like a good shepherd to us, in our life? Share a story of when God was like a shepherd to you. *(Or use a story at parentingforfaith.org/comfort-stories.)*
- The sheep follow the shepherd's voice to stay close to him and it makes them feel safe. How do you stay close to God and feel safe and calm?
- Sometimes when we feel anxious or sad, we really need to be comforted. What do people do to comfort each other and make each other feel better? What do you think God does to comfort us?

Connect with God

Let's connect with God and chat with him about this.

- Shepherds do so much for their sheep. They lead them, find the lost ones, give them what they need, keep them safe. God is our shepherd. What do you really need from God right now? Let's tell him. *(Do this in your head or by whispering into your hands.)*
- God the shepherd is always there and knows what we need right now. Let's close our eyes and ask God to please come close and give us what we need right now. *(Wait ten seconds in quiet.)*
- *You might want to finish with a prayer* – Thank you, God, for being our good shepherd. Guide us, comfort us, hold us and keep us safe. Come and find us when we feel lost. We are so glad that you take care of us.
- *Chat briefly to each other and ask and share* – What do you feel God was doing when we were quiet?

4
Shem
and the long wait

Genesis 6-8

> **KEY TRUTH**
> God is preparing for our future even when we can't see it.

Noah's family was stuck on the water for months and months, with no end in sight. It looked like nothing was happening, and yet God was already preparing a place for them to land and live. Sometimes we can't see what God is doing, and it feels like we are just stuck in the in-between place. But God is working to prepare the next place for us, and we can trust him to know what the next bit will be and what we will need there.

Story

Shem leaned his elbows on the railing of the ark and sighed. The blazing sunlight bounced off the sea, making him squint as he tried to look for land.

And just like every day, all he saw was water, as far as his eyes could see. Water and more water.

Shem started his regular trip around the deck of the huge boat, letting his hand run over the rough wood of the railing as he walked. He kept looking far into the distance, searching for any sign of mountains or islands or trees or anything besides endless ocean.

'Can you see anything exciting?' His mum said as she popped up from a hatch in the deck, carrying a basket of wet clothes.

Shem took the basket out of her hands and helped her up on to the deck. Then he leaned back against the railing. 'I was just hoping that something would happen. That we could get off this boat and start a new life. God saved us from this flood, but that was six months ago. Since then, we've just been here. Floating. Waiting. What's going on?'

'I don't know,' his mum replied. 'God talked to us so clearly about building the boat and gathering the animals that I have to believe he has some sort of plan for our future.'

'Pff, maybe,' said Japheth, Shem's brother, as he climbed up from below deck to join the conversation. 'Or maybe God's waiting for *us* to do something! Maybe we should make a rota to pray day and night for the waters to go away. Or maybe we should tear down some animal stalls and use the wood to make a small boat and search farther out.'

'Make a small boat?' their mum chuckled, as she strung up a rope from railing to railing. 'Now that's a unique idea.' She nudged the basket towards Japheth with her foot, and he started to hang the wet clothes on the line to dry.

'Your father *is* doing something,' she said. 'A couple of weeks ago he sent out that raven to see if it could find land.'

Shem rolled his eyes. 'But that didn't do anything. It just flew around back and forth.'

Japheth hung up another long piece of cloth and said, 'Don't forget the dove. He tried that, and after a week it came back. It couldn't find anywhere to land!'

Their mum smiled. 'Well, your father doesn't give up easily. He sent another dove out this morning.'

Shem frowned. Sending out birds to try to find land didn't seem like a logical way to help. Shem felt trapped, like the animals in the boat.

What if this waiting around in-between-ness went on forever? Where was God and what was he doing while they were all waiting? 'I look out every day and I don't see any change,' said Shem quietly. 'The water is the same. The sky is the same.' He sighed. 'Maybe God forgot us.'

Their mum came over to Shem and looked out across the water. 'Sometimes you can't see what God is doing. That doesn't mean nothing's happening. When I was pregnant with you, God grew you inside my womb for nine whole months. None of us could see what God was doing. We didn't know what your face would look like or what your personality would be like. We couldn't see when you got those super long toes or that funny little way your hair curls up on the side.'

She ruffled Shem's hair. 'We couldn't see anything, but God was doing something amazing.'

Japheth laughed. 'I remember I was so impatient to get to meet you. Every day I'd tell mum to try and push you out. She kept telling me it wasn't time yet, but I didn't care! I wanted to play with you as soon as possible. She kept saying I had to wait because a baby needed all that time to grow.'

Their mum smiled at Japheth. 'I trust that God is doing something, but we just can't see… yet.'

Shem turned to lean against the railing again and the soft breeze blew in his hair. *Could God be doing something right now?* he wondered. A little flicker caught Shem's eye. He stood up straight and squinted into the bright sky. 'Mum? Do you see that?' He pointed towards the billowing clouds.

'Oooh, that cloud looks like a giraffe!'

'No, Mum. That little speck over there. What is *that*?' Shem pointed again. 'Japheth, come look!'

Japheth thumped into place next to them, and they all squinted at the tiny, flitting spot in the sky.

'When did you say Dad sent out that dove?' Shem asked.

'This morning,' their mum replied. 'But I don't know why it would be back so soon. The last dove was gone for much longer. I'll call for your father.' She walked to the hatch and yelled down, 'Noah! Your dove is coming back. Come see.'

Shem watched in fascination as the dove grew bigger and bigger as it came closer.

'Is there something in its mouth?' asked Japheth.

The dove landed on the railing, and Shem gently approached it, trying not to scare it. 'I think it's a small branch with leaves on it,' he said. 'The dove must have found land!'

Japheth gently picked up the dove and held it close to his chest. He carefully removed the branch from its mouth and handed it to Shem. Then he left to return the dove to its cage.

Shem stared at the branch in fascination. It had been six months since he had seen a live plant. To him, all the world was covered in water. But somewhere, God was doing something. The water *was* going down. Land was reappearing. Plants were growing again. Somewhere.

Shem touched the delicate leaf. A whole future was being prepared for them, and he didn't even know it. God hadn't forgotten them. He was getting the world ready for them.

Their mum reached for the branch, and he handed it to her. 'So, what do we do now, Shem?' she asked.

Shem grinned. 'I guess we wait for God to finish what he's working on.'

Conversation starters

Let's answer some questions together. I'll answer them too.

- What part of the story did you like or find interesting or surprising? Why?
- What does this story tell us about God?
- Not a lot of people like waiting. Why is waiting so hard?
- When we can't see what God is doing, we can sometimes think that God has forgotten us. Have you ever felt that God wasn't doing what you wanted him to do?
- What is coming up that you are worried about? What do you hope that God is doing right now, even if you can't see it?

Connect with God

Let's connect with God and chat with him about this.

- God, sometimes it's hard to wait and not know what is next. Thank you that you prepare for our future even when we can't see it. Tell God in your head, or whisper into your hands, what you are worried about for the future.
- Tell God how you feel when you need to wait for him to do something.
- Ask God to give you peace as you trust him to get everything ready for you. *(Wait ten seconds or more.)*
- *You might want to finish with a prayer* – Thank you, God, that even though we can't see it, you are right now doing things to prepare for our future and provide for us right now. We trust that when you are ready, you will bring us right where we need to be to find it. We love you.

5
Pressure in Philippi

Acts 16; Philippians 4:6-7

Anxiety can easily take over our thoughts, making even the smallest challenge seem overwhelming. God doesn't want us to live with that pressure and wants to give us peace even in the most extreme situations. Again and again, we can find God's peace in hard times. In his letter to the house churches in Philippi, Paul shows us how.

Story

'Come in! Come in!'

Charis listened to her father's booming voice as he greeted friends and strangers who came to their home to talk about Jesus. Each week the group would eat a meal, sing and pray, laugh and talk about scripture.

Charis peeked around the thin apricot curtain that separated the back room from the front to see who had arrived today. She normally loved these gatherings, but not today. She had too many other things on her mind.

Her dad was in charge of the small prison in Philippi, and tomorrow she would start bringing the food from her house to the prison so the prisoners could eat.

The more she thought about her new responsibilities, the more she worried. What if the prisoners were mean? What if she tripped and fell on the way and dropped the food? What if she embarrassed herself by saying something stupid in front of the guards her dad worked with? Ugh! Charis took a few deep breaths. She *so* wanted to do well and make her dad proud.

Charis rubbed her aching stomach, but she couldn't get rid of the worry. Just thinking about tomorrow made her feel all jittery inside.

'Charis!' Her father called. 'We're starting soon.'

'Coming.' She sighed and straightened her tunic, and quickly slipped through the curtain into the large, warm front room. She looked around at the sea of faces. She knew some of the people. Others she didn't. Each week it was like that.

Her mum's best friend, Lydia, waved to her from across the room and beckoned her over. 'Charis, I hear tomorrow is your big first day! How exciting! How are you feeling about it?'

'Fine, I guess,' she nodded weakly.

Lydia smiled and touched Charis' cheek. 'Well, I have a surprise tonight that just might help you feel better.' She winked and pointed to the letter in her hand.

Then Lydia straightened up and raised her voice loud above the bustling crowd in the room. 'Everyone! Great news! Today I received a letter from Paul.' She held it up for all to see. 'Now many of you may know Paul already, but some of you may not. He came here to Philippi, oh, around ten years ago, I think.'

'Nine years.' Charis' father jumped in. 'He was in my prison. I remember I was fast asleep when an earthquake shook the place and nearly destroyed my jail. The doors opened, so I thought Paul and Silas had run away. But they hadn't. Instead, they stayed and told us about Jesus, and right there in the middle of the night my whole family learned the truth and got baptised by lamplight!' Her father broke into a huge smile, recalling the happy memory.

Lydia reclaimed the spotlight. 'As you know,' she said, 'Paul is in prison again for talking about Jesus, this time in Rome. It looks like he may not be released. So, this may be the last letter we ever receive from him.'

She pulled up a high stool and sat down, and everyone settled in around the room, including Charis. She picked a chair in the back, away from everyone.

Lydia opened the letter and carefully smoothed out the folds. She said, 'In this letter are the words God gave Paul to write to us. Let me read them to you now.'

Charis listened for quite a while, but she couldn't stay focused. Her mind wandered back to her worries. She pictured all the food she had to cook and the path she would take to the prison. She imagined what the prisoners might say and the mistakes she might make. She worried about it over and over again until the stress of it all came pressing down on her like a heavy duvet. She wanted to cry. And then... Lydia's voice interrupted her thoughts.

Lydia read, 'Don't worry about anything; instead, pray about everything. Tell God what you need, and thank him for all he has done. Then you will experience God's peace, which exceeds anything we can understand. His peace will guard your hearts and minds as you live in Christ Jesus.'*

Those words shook Charis like an earthquake. She knew at that moment she didn't want to forget any of them. She closed her eyes and replayed them in her mind, listening to each part again:

---

* Philippians 4:6–7 (NLT)

Don't worry about anything. Charis wondered how she could possibly do that. She had so much to worry about!

Tell God what you need. She knew this part would be easy because she needed everything! Charis kept her eyes closed and spoke to God in her mind:

God, I need that peace that Paul was talking about. I'm worried I'm not going to be good enough tomorrow, or that I won't do it right. I'm so worried I will let my dad down. I'm scared. I need your strength and truth.

Once Charis started pouring out her heart to God, she couldn't stop. She continued telling him all her feelings and worries until she ran out of words and her mind was finally quiet. She sat back in her chair and leaned her head against the cool wall and rested.

Thank him for all he has done. Charis was ready for this part. She took in a shaky breath and let it out slowly. Then she began to pray: *Thank you God for my family. Thank you for sending Paul to my dad's prison so we could know you. Thank you for this opportunity to help feed people in prison. Thank you for picking us to tell people about you. Thank you for talking to me when I need you. Thank you…*

On and on, the thankfulness overflowed. For every 'thank you' that poured out of Charis, she felt a deep, calm peace pouring back into her body and heart. After a while, she just sat quietly, now knowing the delicious, safe, secure feeling of peace. No worry. No fear. Just peace.

Charis now thought about the last part of Paul's words: *Then you will experience God's peace, which exceeds anything we can understand. His peace will guard your hearts and minds as you live in Christ Jesus.*

Charis smiled. *God, thank you for giving me this peace today. I love that your peace will stand guard over me tomorrow!*

Conversation starters

Let's answer some questions together. I'll answer them too.

- What part of the story did you like or find interesting or surprising? Why?
- What does this story tell us about God?
- Do you ever worry or get anxious? What does it feel like in your brain or body? Why is it so hard to stop that feeling on your own?
- God loves us so much. Why is it so important to God that we not worry or feel anxious?
- Peace is the opposite of worry. Jesus is called the Prince of Peace. What does being peaceful feel like? Can you tell a story of a time when you felt very peaceful?

Connect with God

Let's connect with God and chat with him about this.

- It's hard to stop worrying or feeling anxious. God wants to help. Paul, the person who wrote the letter to Charis and her friends, had been shipwrecked *three times*, yelled at, threatened, put in prison and had lots of other bad things happen to him. He had to learn from God how to find his peace. He told Charis and her friends how to do it. Let's try it together!
- The first part is to tell God everything that is in our heart about how we feel and what we need. Let's chat to God in our heads or whisper into our hands about anything we feel worried or anxious about. He wants to hear it all. Let me know when you are done, take as long as you want. I'll do it too. *(If your child is more visual or physical, enable them to draw or write what they feel.)*
- The next part is to thank God for all he has been doing. Let's do that now. What has God been doing? What is true and good about… *(fill in the situation they are in)*? If you aren't sure, we can do it together or separately.

- The last part is to enjoy God's peace. God, we've told you all that's in our hearts, and thanked you for all you are and all you are doing. Thank you for your peace now, God. Let's be quiet for a little bit and breathe deeply as God gives us his peace. *(Wait ten or more seconds with God.)*
- *You may want to finish with a prayer* – Thank you, God, that you want to always give us peace. Thank you for helping us put down what gets us stuck so we can look to you. Guard our hearts and minds with your peace today, God.
- *Chat to each other briefly about your experience* – How was that? How do you feel now?

6

The five sisters
and the unfair law

Numbers 27:1-11

KEY TRUTH

God loves justice, and sometimes in uncertainty we need to speak up for what is right.

Uncertainty can make all of us feel helpless. God often invites us to be bold to speak for what is right when situations happen that are unfair. The five sisters were in deep grief. They had lost their father, and now their future home was being taken away from them just because they weren't men. They could have just sat down in sadness and given up, but they didn't. They knew God loved justice and so fought for the law to change. Sometimes, we have to choose bravery in uncertainty.

Note for parents: We will be using words like 'unfair' and 'wrong' to help process the emotions that your children are feeling. Often children in grief or change may feel a sense of powerlessness and injustice, and they don't quite know how to find the words to express that. As you use the conversations and prayer, you might want to be aware of helping your children express those feelings and help them see God's understanding and opportunities for them to help themselves and others.

Story

The wind blew Tirzah's hair across her face as she nudged a rock with her foot. The desert was hot today, and she was trying to stay out of the way of her big sister Hoglah, who was under great stress. Today was the big day when her little family of five sisters would attempt to save the future of their family. If they could all get in one place, that is.

'Girls, please come over here!' Hoglah stomped towards her younger siblings who were playing in the dirt next to a row of tents.

Tirzah sighed and put her eye up to the crack in the long fence that surrounded the courtyard of God's tent. It was made of rough wood frames holding huge pieces of white fabric that billowed in the wind. If she positioned her head just right, she could see what was going on inside.

Through the small space, she could see Moses himself talking to the priests, and many men walking around. All the big, in-charge people of her community were there. Her mouth went dry with nervousness.

She felt her sister Hoglah come up behind her to look through the fence too.

'I still don't think we should do this!' Tirzah whispered. 'If God wanted the law changed, then wouldn't he just change it? We can't do anything to fix this. They aren't going to listen to us.'

Hoglah shook her head. 'When father died, we lost more than him. We lost our future. The law says we can't get any of our father's land or belongings when we go into the promised land because we're women. It'll be like father never existed. We won't have anything to live on to bring to our future families. We will be homeless. It is so wrong!'

Tirzah turned to her sister. 'I know it's wrong. But do you really think *those* guys,' Tirzah pointed toward the courtyard, 'are going to look at a small family of women and say, "Oh, sure we'll change the law for you?"' Tirzah shook her head. 'They'll just send us away.'

Hoglah adjusted her tunic roughly. 'Not if I persuade them.' Hoglah leaned in to look through the fence again. Her face turned a little bit white. 'Everybody important is in there.'

Tirzah looked at Hoglah. 'God will teach you what to say.'

They huddled together briefly and whispered a short prayer: 'God, please help us.'

With a final squeeze, the five sisters walked through the entrance into the courtyard.

Tirzah looked around cautiously, and she could feel her hands getting sweaty. She wasn't even sure if they were allowed in there. No one noticed them yet, so Hoglah tugged on her sleeve and said, 'Let's go,' and started to weave through the crowd towards Moses.

As they walked, the priests and leaders began to notice them, and they started talking among themselves and pointing. Tirzah glanced over at Hoglah, and saw her lips moving as she practised what she wanted to say to convince the leaders.

Ahead, God's tent came into view as they walked closer. Tirzah's heart began to thump loudly in her chest as she saw Moses talking with the priests. These were the people who would decide whether they would have a home or not.

Tirzah glanced up to the cloud of God in the sky above the tent. She didn't trust that these people would listen to her, but she knew that her family wasn't alone. Throughout these years in the desert God frequently talked about fairness and justice. He often commanded their community to ensure that people were treated fairly. She looked around the courtyard. Maybe their family wasn't the only one here seeking justice. Maybe God would be too.

Moses looked up and saw them. He paused what he was saying, and his look of surprise softened to a kind smile. 'Hello! I'm Moses. How can I help you?'

Tirzah could feel Hoglah shaking a bit beside her, so she stepped for-ward and squeezed Hoglah's hand. Hoglah squeezed back and spoke up so all could hear: 'Our father died while we were travelling through the desert. He *didn't* die in the rebellion. He just died because he was old. He didn't have any sons, just us five daughters. The law says that our uncles will get our father's land, because girls can't inherit their father's land. But we think that's wrong. We want our father to be remembered and to carry on his name on his land.'

Moses' face was filled with concern. 'Please wait here. I will go and talk with God about this. It is *his* law after all.' Moses waved his hand to the surrounding priests and leaders to be patient as he slipped into the tent of God.

Tirzah whispered 'Well done!' to her sister and gave her a small smile. 'Now we wait.'

Tirzah felt like everyone was staring at them, as she and her four sisters stood in a little clump in front of God's tent, waiting to see what God said. Tirzah looked at the faces of her littler sisters, and prayed for God to save them from an uncertain future.

A few minutes later, the tent flap opened and Moses emerged. He spoke quietly to a nearby priest, who called out loudly, 'Everyone gather around to hear the judgement of God.'

Tirzah didn't know whether that was a good thing or a bad thing. She tried to search Moses' face for any clues of what he was going to say, but she couldn't tell.

Moses raised his hands for quiet. 'I brought this family's case to the Lord, and this is what he said.' Moses paused and a smile spread across his face. 'The Lord said, "The daughters of Zelophehad are right. They should share the land with their father's brothers. So give them the land that you would have given to their father."'

'Thank you, God!' Tirzah's hands flew up in the air in celebration, and Hoglah flung her arms around her younger sisters as they cheered. God had heard them. God *agreed* with them!

Tirzah heard the murmurs among the leaders standing around. Some were not taking this news well, but she didn't care. Relief flooded her whole body. She and her sisters would have a future among her people just like her father wanted. God really was a God of justice!

Out of the corner of her eye, Tirzah saw Moses waving for quiet. She was confused. It appeared Moses had more to say. Maybe God had more to say.

Moses continued: 'God then said to me, "If a man has no son, when he dies everything he owns will be given to his daughter. If he has no daughter, everything he owns will be given to his brothers… This will be a law among the Israelites."'

As Moses continued on, Tirzah couldn't believe what she was hearing. God didn't just help their little family. God seemed to be changing the way all daughters would be treated forever. Tirzah looked around at the astonished faces in the courtyard. Everyone would be affected by this law. Justice would come to generations of women for hundreds of years in the future.

Tirzah knelt on the hard ground in front of God's cloud, and she felt her sisters follow. She was overwhelmed with what God was doing. *We are just five people who thought something was wrong, and said so. Look what God can do when someone stands up. Thank you, God. Thank you, God.*

And God's quiet voice whispered to her, *Well done*.

Conversation starters

Let's answer some questions together. I'll answer them too.

- What part of the story did you like or find interesting or surprising? Why?
- What does this story tell us about God?
- Sometimes our situations feel very unfair, like something wrong is being done to us. Can you think of a time when you felt that? I'll go first. *(Or use a story at **parentingforfaith.org/comfort-stories**.)*
- In this story, the sisters felt they had to be brave to stand up for themselves and say what was wrong. Why is it so hard to be brave and say something when situations feel unfair?
- God helped the sisters and then used their bravery to change the law forever, for all women. What feels unfair about… *(fill in the situation your child is in)*? What difference could you and God make to yourself and others if you got brave? What would you like to do?

Connect with God

Let's connect with God and chat with him about this.

- Let's tell God in our heads or whisper into our hands what we think is unfair in… *(fill in the situation)* and how it makes us feel.
- God, we want to stand up when we feel something is wrong. You say you love justice and bringing rightness to the world. Please drop your ideas into our minds and hearts right now and over the coming days. I want to be brave. Fill us with your courage to speak and do. *(Wait ten or more seconds with God.)*
- *You may want to finish with a prayer* – Thank you, God, that you care about what is right. You made our mouths and bodies. Teach us what to say and fill us with your bravery and strength, so that we can stand up for ourselves and others. We love you, God.
- *Chat about how you want to capture the ideas that you have now and will have next and what you want to do about it.*

7

Singing in a cave

1 Samuel 22:1; Psalm 51

Music is a powerful gift. It can change the way we feel and can give us words to express ourselves better than we thought we could. Throughout history, people have been singing songs to God to connect to him. When we sing to God, it can replace fear with truth and sweep away worry. Even in huge change, anxiety or grief, worship music can help us express ourselves to God and connect to him.

Story

David steadied himself against the rocky hillside and carefully scanned the terrain below and around him. He stared intently at every shadow, looking for any movement. He had to make sure no one was following him. What was the point of hiding if people knew where you were?

David turned and braced his hands against the cave's entrance and peered in. He strained to see inside, but all he saw was darkness. He listened intently for a minute or two, making sure he didn't hear any growls or breathing. Nothing. Just silence. Maybe this cave *would* work, he thought.

David glanced back one more time, then ducked inside, his feet slipping over some loose rocks. Then he stood up warily, letting his eyes adjust to the dim light. He cautiously stepped deeper in, until he found a spot with a flat floor and tall sloping walls. David nodded. This was the spot. King Saul wouldn't find him here.

David kicked a few stones aside, rolled out his blanket on the floor and sat down. He leaned against a large rock and stared at nothing in particular. Then he thought about his life. It certainly wasn't going the way *he* had planned. Years ago, God's prophet told him he'd be king one day. It all sounded so great back then. He fought Goliath and served King Saul the best he could. He worked hard to be ready for the day he'd be king.

But then it all went so wrong. And now for some reason the king *really* hated him and was out to get him. Of all the ways he thought his life would go, running from a king and hiding in a cave definitely were *not* among them.

The air was quiet. David shifted his body to get more comfortable, and then he sighed. He listened to the questions piling up in his mind, and he prayed them to God: *Why did things go so wrong? What do you want me to do? How can I be king if I'm living in a cave?*

David threw up his arms in sadness and confusion. No one knew he was here. No one could help. Except God, of course.

David tossed a stone against the far wall and listened to it *ping* and tumble to the ground. He closed his eyes and decided to sing. Singing had always comforted him.

He sang a song from his childhood when he watched his father's sheep back home. David loved the melody, but the words were all wrong for how he felt now. He needed new words.

He decided to hum the song this time, listening to its melody, and choosing new words. His own words. Words that came right from his heart to God: 'Have mercy on me, O God, have mercy! I look to you for protection. I will hide beneath the shadow of your wings until the danger passes by.'*

_____

*   Psalm 57:1 (NLT)

David liked how the words sounded when he sung them, so he sang them again. He imagined himself hiding safely in God's arms. As he sang, the tension in his body relaxed and slowly slipped away. He was feeling safe again.

The safer he felt, the more he wanted to sing. And then David realised something else. He couldn't make himself into a king, no matter what he did. It was God's plan all along. Not his. So, God would have to work it out.

David smiled and found more words for his song: 'I cry out to God Most High, to the God who will fulfil his purpose for me. My heart is confident in you, O God; my heart is confident. No wonder I can sing your praises!'*

David's heart was ablaze with love for God. He jumped up and sang his song from beginning to end, as loud as he could. And he ended with more new words:

'I will sing your praises among the nations. For your unfailing love is as high as the heavens. Your faithfulness reaches to the clouds.'

David's voice echoed through the cave as if angels were singing with him. He lay down on his blanket and closed his eyes, taking in a long, grateful breath. The worries were gone from his heart.

The God who loved him *was* keeping him safe, and *would* be faithful to do what he said he would do.

He took another deep breath, and began to sing to God again.

---

* Psalm 57:2, 7 (NLT)

Conversation starters

Let's answer some questions together. I'll answer them too.

- What part of the story did you like or find interesting or surprising? Why?
- What does this story tell us about God?
- What are some of your favourite songs right now? Why do you like them so much? How do they make you feel when you listen to them?
- David loved singing songs to God, when he was happy and sad, scared and joyful. Why do you think God designed music to be so powerful to humans?
- What are some of your favourite worship songs? How do they help you connect with God?

Connect with God

Let's connect with God and chat with him about this.

- Let's spend some time just worshipping God together. I'll start by praying, and then if a worship song pops into your head, or if you have a song you really want to listen to that will help you express yourself to God or remind you of a truth, we'll listen to it on my phone. If I can't find it, we can just sing it the best we can!
- God, you know our situation. Let's chat to God about how we are feeling in our head or whisper to God into our hands. *(Wait for a few seconds to do that.)* We want to be with you and meet with you about it through music. Remind us of songs that will help us connect with you.
- *Have everybody feel free to make requests, or start singing. You can lie down and listen to the songs or sing along, whatever you feel most comfortable doing. Some kids may want to draw or write while listening to the songs. Take turns letting people choose what songs they want. Feel free to stop when you feel it's the right time.*

- *You may want to finish with a prayer* – Thank you, God, that as we sing to you, you come close and our hearts are lifted to you. We love you.

Make a playlist

- *At a different time, you may want to create a playlist of songs that help your family in this particular situation. Ask your family what worship songs remind them of the truth you all need to hear, help bring joy and peace to their hearts, or express what they feel to God or about God.*
- *Play that playlist in the car or in your home. Add to it as you all discover new songs, and start a new playlist when a new season comes.*

8

The fourth man

Daniel 1-3

KEY TRUTH

God is with us at all times, whether or not we can see him.

It is easy to feel alone when we experience grief, anxiety or change. The most common promise in scripture is that God will be with us, and yet we often don't feel it. Shadrach, Meshach and Abednego were three friends who had lived through a lot. They survived a war as children, were captured and moved thousands of miles away, and now they were trying to serve God surrounded by people who had a different religion to them. But they knew that God was with them in the difficulty and took comfort in that, even if he didn't rescue them.

Story

Abednego pulled his thick cloak tight around him. The cold breeze made him shiver. He and his friends had started early on their walk to Dura, but even after a few hours, the air was still chilly.

'Okay, okay, my turn to choose,' said Abednego. He grinned at his two friends. 'Next target is… that tree. Who can throw a rock and hit the highest point on that tree?' He pointed at the tall, twisted one on the other side of the road.

Shadrach laughed and picked up a rock near his foot. He aimed carefully, and let it fly.

'It missed!' Meshach crowed.

'It hit the little branches on the side!' said Shadrach, confidently. 'Come on then. Your go!'

Abednego smiled as they went back and forth. He was so grateful for his friends. He had known them for years, since they were young. They were all captured and brought here together to Babylon after the war. And through it all, they stayed friends. Now they were grown and had important jobs in the government, overseeing an entire region of the king's land.

Abednego loved how they still worshipped the one true God, even though they lived in Babylon. It wasn't always easy. Over the years they had to make tough choices to keep themselves, and each other, close to God, especially since most people in Babylon didn't know him. Meshach would always encourage them to keep seeking God and not give up. Shadrach always found some scripture to remind them of God's truth. And God always made them feel as if his right hand was on their backs, as if he were with them every step of the way. They made a good team.

'Look at that!' Meshach said, pointing ahead.

Off in the distance was a huge, glittering gold statue of their king. The sun glinted off it with such force, they almost had to squint to look at it. Around the statue's base were people walking around. They looked as small as ants.

'It's so much bigger than I thought it would be,' said Shadrach.

Meshach nodded. 'Well, the king wanted every official person in government to come here and see it completed.'

Abednego felt worried. *Okay, God*, he prayed. *We really need your wisdom on this one. Stand really close to us. We need you.* 'Come on,' he said. 'Looks like they're getting ready to start the ceremony. We shouldn't be late.'

As they got closer, they made their way to an open area in front of the gold statue and looked up. It was so enormous they weren't even tall enough to reach its toes. To the side of the statue was a group of musicians warming up. On a higher platform were members of the royal court milling around. Abednego couldn't see the king, but he knew he was there somewhere.

Shadrach sniffed the air. 'Do you smell smoke?' He glanced around. 'Look, it's coming from over there.' Behind the statue, a strand of thick black smoke curved its way into the sky.

Abednego felt uncomfortable. Something just didn't feel right. 'Let's go to the back and stand behind the crowd.'

Meshach nodded. 'I agree.'

They wove their way quietly to a place near the back.

Shadrach studied the statue from head to toe. 'It really does look like the king,' he whispered.

Drums sounded out, calling the people to attention. The crowd quietened down. A herald stood up on the platform next to the statue, and his voice rang out clearly across the audience.

'All you people from many nations and language groups, listen to me. This is what you are commanded to do: You must bow down as soon as you hear all the musical instruments… You must worship the gold idol. King Nebuchadnezzar has set this idol up. Whoever does not bow down and worship this gold idol will immediately be thrown into a very hot furnace.'

Abednego's stomach felt like it sunk to the floor. *God, oh, God. What do we do?* He turned to his friends in shock. 'We can't worship this statue.'

Shadrach shook his head. 'No way. God clearly tells us in his word: "You must not worship any other gods except me."'*

Meshach's hands were shaking. 'This isn't the first time we've been faced with a decision like this,' he said. 'We have to serve God first. We can do this.'

Abednego grabbed his friends' arms and quietly prayed, 'God, we know you are with us always. Stand close to us now. We love you, God, and we choose you.'

Immediately Abednego felt steadier. Whatever happened next, he knew the truth deep in his mind and heart, that God himself would be with them, standing among them.

Abednego looked at his friends a final time, and then the music began to play. In a rush of noise, hundreds of people around them knelt on the ground and touched their foreheads to the dirt. They stretched their arms out in front of them and worshipped the enormous gold idol of the king, as if it were God.

Abednego stood still, alongside his friends. No one around them seemed to notice they weren't kneeling. Abednego began to wonder if God had hidden them from sight.

Meshach raised his eyebrows and glanced side to side as the music ended and the people began to stand.

Abednego breathed a sigh of relief. 'Well, somehow we made it through that!' he said.

Shadrach's face crumpled with concern. 'I'm not so sure. I saw some movement on the royal platform that didn't look good. Let's get out of here.'

---

* Exodus 20:3

Just then a small man in a deep red robe shouted and pointed at Abednego and his friends. Then guards quickly appeared out of the crowd and rushed towards them.

Within minutes the three friends were escorted up to king, in the shadow of the statue. He was dressed in his best robes and looked angry.

The king roared, 'Is it true that you didn't bow down and worship the gold idol I have set up?' He paced back and forth angrily, and then took a few deep breaths. Abednego knew that they were valuable to the king. They did their jobs well, and the king was pleased with them, normally. Maybe he would spare them.

The king lowered his voice and spoke slowly: 'Now, when you hear the sound of the musical instruments, you must bow down and worship the gold idol. If you are ready to worship the idol I have made, that is good. But if you don't worship it, you will be thrown very quickly into the hot furnace. Then no god will be able to save you from my power!'

Shadrach turned and whispered to Abednego, 'God says in his word: "Remember, I commanded you to be strong and brave. Don't be afraid, because the Lord your God will be with you wherever you go."'*

The king glared at Shadrach and took three steps towards them. He leaned in close. '*What* did you say? I told you to bow down to my idol!'

Anger began to grow in Abednego, as if God himself was pouring courage into his heart. *The king thinks he's mightier than God. He isn't!* Abednego pulled his shoulders back and looked straight into the king's eyes.

'King Nebuchadnezzar, we don't need to explain ourselves to you,' he said. The guards gasped at his words. 'If you throw us into the hot

---

* Joshua 1:9

furnace, the God we serve can save us. And if he wants to, he can save us from your power. But even if God does not save us, we want you to know, King, that we refuse to serve your gods. We will not worship the gold idol you have set up.'

The king's face turned a terrible red, and he yelled at the guards: 'Make the fire seven times hotter! Tie them up and throw them into the furnace!'

The king's guards leaped forward and tied up Abednego and his friends. As they were dragged toward the furnace, Abednego felt strangely peaceful.

'God is with us!' called out Meshach.

The mouth of the furnace was opened wide. The fire was blazing inside, with flames leaping taller than the three of them. The heat was so intense that Abednego felt as if he were being thrown into the sun. Abednego closed his eyes. *I love you, God.*

Then he felt a shove on his back, and he fell forward into the fiery furnace.

He landed on the ground with a thud.

He kept his eyes closed and waited. Was this what dying felt like? He felt no pain. He felt no heat. He opened his eyes slowly. All around he saw flames towering above him, smouldering beneath him. He was *in* the fire and yet he was unharmed. His hands and legs were no longer tied up. How was this possible?

He reached out to his friends laying on the ground next to him. 'Shadrach! Meshach!' he called out as he shook them.

They opened their eyes slowly and looked at Abednego, and then at the flames. 'What's happening?' asked Meshach.

'This must be God's doing,' said Shadrach, his eyes now wide open.

They helped each other up, and felt each other's robes and hair. Nothing was burnt. No one was hurt. They began to laugh with joy and burst into praise, shouting, 'The Lord God is saving us! He is the one true God!'

'He really *is* with us!' said Abednego.

Then a voice behind them said, 'Yes, I am.'

They turned around to see a figure brighter than anything they had ever seen before. He was in the midst of the fire *with* them, and he was smiling.

Abednego didn't want to move. 'God is with us,' he sighed, overwhelmed with love and gratefulness.

King Nebuchadnezzar's voice broke through the roar of the flames: 'Shadrach, Meshach and Abednego, come out! Servants of the Most High God, come here!'

The figure nodded at Abednego, and he knew God wanted them to go out to the king. Abednego gently tugged on his friends' arms and said, 'Let's go. We have more to do.' They smiled and agreed.

And after one final look at the figure, Abednego stepped out of the furnace and walked towards the king. He had just seen with his own eyes the God who had been with him his whole life. He knew, deep in his heart, that this same God would be with him and his children forever, whether they could see him or not.

Conversation starters

Let's answer some questions together. I'll answer them too.

- What part of the story did you like or find interesting or surprising? Why?
- What does this story tell us about God?
- God was with the three friends for their whole lives through the war, their capture and even in the furnace. They knew he was there in different ways. How do you know that God is with you?
- God didn't rescue them from war, but the three friends still loved and trusted God. Why?
- Why does knowing that God is with you make a difference?
- Tell a story of when you needed to know God was with you and it really helped you in the situation. (*Or use a story at parentingforfaith.org/comfort-stories.*)

Connect with God

Let's connect with God and chat with him about this.

- God has been with you for your whole life. Can you show God a memory or tell him a memory of a time that you knew he was with you?
- God has memories of being with you too. Let's ask God to remind us of a time that he really liked being with us. (*Wait ten seconds or more.*)
- Sometimes we need help to remember that God is with us. Let's think of a special signal that we can do with God that no one will know about, that can say to God at any time, 'Hi! I'm glad you are here.' It can be a finger wiggle, a secret tap, a wink, anything you and God want. Chat with him and decide.
- Tell God about a situation or place where you really want to know that he is with you.

- *You may want to finish with a prayer* – God, thank you for being with us and helping us. I love that we do not have to feel alone, but in every situation you are right by our side helping us along. Help us know that you are with us in all times, especially when we feel uncertain.
- *Encourage your family to do the signal to God at least once today.*

9
Martha
and the bad day

Luke 10:38-42

KEY TRUTH

God invites us to stop doing and rest with him.

Sometimes when we feel uncertain about life, we can fill up our brains and hearts with business: homework, games, classes, social media, TV and YouTube. We can want to control everything around us and then feel stressed when it doesn't all work. God has a different way to help us. He asks us to put it down and enjoy time with him.

Story

'Lazarus, can you come out for a minute, please?' Martha called to her brother.

It was warm in the courtyard, and sitting by the cooking fire made the heat even worse. Martha wiped the sweat off her forehead with the back of her hand, and then scraped the freshly chopped vegetables into the bubbling stew. She tried to think of what she had to do next. All the different chores kept swirling in her mind.

Her guests laughed loudly in the house, but she couldn't see them. She wished she could hear what they were laughing about.

Martha stirred the stew and sighed. She loved when Jesus and his disciples dropped by. She always wanted them to feel welcome in her home. But it was not easy cooking for 20 people, not to mention making sure they had enough to drink and places to sleep if they wanted to stay.

Martha stopped stirring, and she put the lid back on the pot. She moved over to the small oven to start baking bread. Her chest felt tight with stress. It was dinner time. Her friends would be hungry, but she hadn't finished cooking. She sighed. She hated feeling like a failure. Especially when all the work was for Jesus.

Her brother stepped into the courtyard and squinted in the sunlight. 'What's up?' he asked.

She pointed to the stone pitchers on the side table. 'Would you please take those in and make sure the guests have enough to drink? I keep forgetting to do it.'

'Don't worry about the guests,' said Lazarus. 'They're having a good time. Jesus is telling stories.'

Martha's lower lip began to quiver. She loved Jesus' stories, and she was missing out on them. If only she could work faster, then she could finish her chores and get in there to hear a few of them.

Martha took a piece of soft dough and flattened it between her hands. 'Where's Mary? I asked her to help chop vegetables and bake flat bread, but she's disappeared. I really need her help here!'

Lazarus hesitated.

Martha squinted her eyes at him and repeated her question: 'Where is Mary?'

'She's sitting, listening to Jesus.'

Martha took a deep breath and exhaled hard. So, Mary was sitting and listening to Jesus *instead* of helping her! Martha let that hurtful thought sink down to her heart. She flattened another piece of dough and slapped it into the oven. 'Please take the drinks. The guests must be thirsty by now.'

Lazarus agreed. He swept up the pitchers in both hands and headed back into the house. Martha could hear the thankful cheers erupt as he entered. She stood still for a moment and listened to the happiness in the house. Then she wanted to cry.

Martha spun around and threw her hands on her hips. She stared at the half-finished chores in front of her. She had more vegetables to chop, more pots to stir and the rest of the dough to make into bread. The chores seemed to never end, and she was irritated she'd have to do them alone.

'Smells good!' said a voice in the doorway.

Martha looked up to see Jesus smiling at her. And without even thinking, she exploded: 'Lord, don't you care that my sister has left me to do all this work by myself? Tell her to help me!' Martha paused, wide-eyed, and tried to gulp back her words. She had just snapped at Jesus.

He stepped towards her, and his voice was gentle. 'Martha, you are worried and upset about so many things.'

She nodded several times. Jesus always seemed to understand. He looked around the courtyard and then back at Martha. 'There is only one thing worth being concerned about. Mary has discovered it, and it will not be taken away from her.'*

Only one thing? thought Martha. She could think of a million things to be concerned about right now. And Mary wasn't helping with any of them. Mary just cared about being with Jesus.

Martha heard her own thoughts and stopped. *Yes, that was it!* Mary just cared about being with Jesus! It all made sense now. Martha looked into Jesus' eyes and sighed. 'Mary is doing what I've been *wanting* to do all day,' she said.

---

* Luke 10:42 (NLT)

Jesus smiled and waved at the food and chaos in the courtyard. 'All that can wait. Come inside.' He headed back to the door.

And right then, the stress in Martha's body seemed to fly up and away, bit by bit. There was only one thing that mattered to her right now: Jesus was in her house, talking and laughing and telling stories, and *she wanted to be with him*.

She could finish cooking later. Others could get the house in order later. It didn't have to be *her* doing all the work. But right now, she knew where she needed to be.

Martha quickly grabbed the cooked bread from the oven, and she pulled the pots farther away from the fire so they would cook more slowly. She smiled at all the mess and the chores waiting to be done, and said to herself, 'It can wait. I need to be with Jesus now.' She turned and sprinted into the house.

As Martha stepped in, the group greeted her and made space for her to sit. Jesus grinned at her, and Mary gave a little wave. As Martha relaxed on the bench, a little flutter of joy lit up her heart. She could feel the peace of God soothe her tired body.

I'll get back to the food soon. But for now, I just need to pause and enjoy Jesus.

Jesus laughed at something Lazarus asked and said, 'Have I ever told you about the first time Andrew took me fishing?' A roar of laughter erupted from the crowd. And as others called for the story, Martha began to smile for the first time that day.

Conversation starters

Let's answer some questions together. I'll answer them too.

- What part of the story did you like or find interesting or surprising? Why?
- What does this story tell us about God?
- Do you ever feel overwhelmed? When? What does it feel like in your body or brain?
- What do you do when you feel overwhelmed?
- Jesus wanted to help Martha, but he didn't rush in to be busy with her. He invited her to relax and be with him. For Mary, it was sitting and listening to Jesus talk and tell stories. But everyone is different. Some people like riding bikes with God, painting with God, dancing with God, reading their Bible or napping with God, or singing or listening to music with God. What do you like to do with God? If you aren't sure, what would you like to try?
- How do you know when you need to stop and rest with God? Tell a story of when you knew and how it helped. *(Or use a story at parentingforfaith.org/comfort-stories.)*

Connect with God

Let's connect with God and chat with him about this.

- Sometimes we all feel overwhelmed. Tell God why you sometimes feel overwhelmed.
- *Everyone is different. Put on a song to create some space for people to think. Think with God about places and ways you can rest together. Share your ideas with God. Ask him to inspire your thoughts as you think together. Make a list!*
- *If you have the time, why not try it out now in private, with no one watching, just you and God? Or decide as a family to have a go privately and then chat about how it went in a few days' time.*

- *You may want to finish with a prayer* – Thank you, God, that you call us to stop and rest with you. You don't want us to live overwhelmed. Thank you for inviting us to be with you and spend time with you, the king of all the universe. It is so wonderful to be loved by you.

10

The desk of the king

2 Kings 19:14-37

KEY TRUTH
God listens and responds.

When situations feel so big, we can want God to swoop in and save us. God always responds to our prayers, in many different ways. Sometimes he does miraculously step in and help us, and other times he steps close to us to help us through. He always responds when we talk to him, and he wants us to bring our enormous requests to him. Nothing is too big to ask. We have seen in the Bible and in our lives how he can make the impossible happen. He listens to our prayers and always responds.

Story

King Hezekiah pushed the scroll back to his secretary and rubbed his eyes. 'Why is there so much paperwork in running a kingdom?' he asked, already knowing the answer. It had been a long day.

Shebna bowed subtly. 'I have one more scroll for you today, my king.' He laid the last one on Hezekiah's desk and spread it out for the king to see. Then he described the request: 'A local family is asking permission to expand their home against the city wall. Most of their family was killed in the battle of Lachish. The remaining children and grandparents are coming to live with them here in Jerusalem. They need to build more rooms.' Shebna pointed to a section in the scroll. 'We need your decision on their request.'

Hezekiah felt his heart sink. Too many families were being destroyed in this war. He looked at the scroll again. The family would definitely need more rooms. 'Give them permission to build against the wall, and use the treasury to pay for it.'

Shebna raised his eyebrows in a look of surprise.

'I can't fix the war,' sighed Hezekiah, 'but I can help with this.' The king grabbed a small piece of paper and scribbled a note on it. 'Please make sure the family gets this note too. I want to make sure they hear directly from their king about this request. I want them to feel heard.'

Shebna rolled up the scroll and took the king's note. 'Thank you, my lord. They will be so happy.'

The door opened, and a messenger slipped into the room. He walked straight past Shebna and knelt near the king. 'A message from Sennacherib, king of Assyria,' he said, as he held out the scroll.

Hezekiah felt a heaviness overwhelm him. He took the scroll and set it down on his desk and thought for a minute. He was losing the war with Assyria, and many of his people were being killed or captured. Sennacherib wanted to control all of Hezekiah's kingdom, even Jerusalem.

Hezekiah let out a long sigh and slowly opened the scroll. This would *not* be good news.

His stomach tightened as he began to read Sennacherib's letter:

'Hezekiah, king of Judah, don't be fooled by the god you trust. Don't believe him when he says Jerusalem will not be handed over to the king of Assyria. You have heard what the kings of Assyria have done. They have completely defeated every country, so do not think you will be saved. Did the gods of those people save them? My ancestors destroyed them. Where are those kings now?'

Hezekiah dropped his face into his hands. He felt lost. He had done everything he could to prepare his city for war with Assyria; he had built walls and towers, and channelled fresh water into the city. But that wouldn't be enough to save Jerusalem and protect his people. The Assyrian army was too big and too vicious.

Hezekiah leaned back in his chair and looked up at Shebna, still standing there holding the bundle of scrolls from that morning. They were filled with so many needs. So many requests for help! Hezekiah answered them the best he could. But he was only a king, not God.

And in that instant, he *knew* what he had to do.

Hezekiah held up the letter and announced to Shebna, 'I'm going to show this to God.' He grabbed his cloak and headed for the door.

'You are going to *show* it to God?' asked Shebna. 'I don't understand.'

Hezekiah didn't answer. He left the palace and stepped on to the busy streets of Jerusalem. He looked up the hill to God's temple, to where God's throne was on earth. That's where he needed to go.

He walked through the streets towards the temple, and his heart ached more and more. All these people could be killed or captured. *O God, hear me. Save your people, God, because I can't.*

As he entered the temple area, a priest on duty stood up in surprise. 'Your majesty! I didn't know you were coming. How can I help you?'

Hezekiah waved an acknowledgement. 'Thank you, but only God can help me.'

The priest bowed. 'You are welcome to God's house, O King.'

Hezekiah strode across the clean white stones, passing priests and others talking and praying. He continued through the inner courtyard, and knelt on the grand steps leading up to the temple doors. He may be a king, but he was here to talk to the king of kings.

Hezekiah bowed before God and took out the small scroll from Sennacherib. He leaned forward and spread out the letter for God to see. Fear and worry and hope all fought inside him. With his hands on the letter and head bowed, he prayed.

'Lord, only you are God of all the kingdoms of the earth. I know you love us, God, and so I have a request.'

He pushed the letter forward towards the doors of the temple and let his head sink to his chest. 'The king of Assyria sent us this letter to threaten us. We aren't strong enough to defend ourselves when they attack. Only you can save us from his power. Please, God save us.'

Hezekiah fell silent. He had brought the letter and his request to the king of kings. Now he would wait for *his* decision. Hezekiah sat quietly on the steps, sometimes praying, sometimes just sitting patiently. He knew that God might not answer right away. He smiled and thought, *You can't rush a king.*

He watched the priests moving around the court with purpose, serving God the best they could. He loved being in the courts of God's temple. His mind thought back to the letter. *Please don't let Sennacherib destroy this place*, he prayed. He thought about leaving and going back to the palace, but he felt peaceful here, and so he stayed. And waited.

In a while, the slapping sounds of running feet interrupted Hezekiah's peace. He turned to see a red-faced young man dash into the courtyard and ask a priest a question. The priest craned his head around and pointed to the king.

Hezekiah glanced down at the letter he had placed before God, and then stood to receive the message.

The young man bowed. 'A message from Isaiah the prophet for you, King Hezekiah.' He took a deep breath and continued: 'The Lord, the God of Israel says: I have heard your prayer concerning Sennacherib,

king of Assyria. This is the word that the Lord has spoken against him.'
The messenger handed Hezekiah a scroll.

Hezekiah's hands were shaking as he opened it to read aloud the words of his heavenly king.

'This is what the Lord says about the king of Assyria: His armies will not enter Jerusalem. They will not even shoot an arrow at it. They will not march outside its gates with their shields nor build banks of earth against its walls.'

Hezekiah's voice trembled as he gulped back tears. He read more: 'The king will return to his own country by the same road on which he came. He will not enter this city, says the Lord. For my own honour and for the sake of my servant David, I will defend this city and protect it.'*

Hezekiah slowly sat down and let his body slump forward, resting his forehead on his knees. His heart celebrated with tears of thankfulness. God had heard him. God had listened. The king of kings had seen his need.

His people would be saved. The temple would be safe.

Hezekiah sighed and looked up at the temple. *What a God we serve! The king of kings who loves us and listens to our needs, and answers.*

Hezekiah knelt to pick up the letter he had placed before God. He wrapped the words of God's answer around it and held it to his chest. *Thank you.*

---

* 2 Kings 19:32–34 (NLT)

Conversation starters

Let's answer some questions together. I'll answer them too.

- What part of the story did you like or find interesting or surprising? Why?
- What does this story tell us about God?
- King Hezekiah's enemy was going to win the war because they were bigger and stronger. The enemy was also trying to convince Hezekiah that God couldn't help him. Why didn't Hezekiah just give up? What made Hezekiah keep hoping that it wasn't all over?
- Hezekiah brought the scary letter to God to show it to him. We know that God is with us everywhere and that he can see everything, but Hezekiah chose to bring the letter and spread it out before God. Why do you think he would do that?
- God responded to Hezekiah after a while. It wasn't straightaway. Hezekiah had to wait to know what God was going to do or say. Do you find it hard to wait for God's response when you chat to him or ask him to do things? Why? What do you feel or think?
- God responded from an outside place. He told his answer to a friend, who then sent God's response to Hezekiah through a messenger. Sometimes God responds to us in ways we don't expect. Share a story of a time God communicated with you in a way that surprised you! *(Or use a story at* **parentingforfaith.org/ comfort-stories.***)*

Connect with God

Let's connect with God and chat with him about this.

- Let's try bringing our big requests to God like Hezekiah! What is your big request to God about… *(fill in the situation that you are in)*? Go find something that you can touch that reminds you of that big request and bring it back here. You may want to save it and do it in private, depending on what you prefer.

- Hold it for a moment, and then put it down in front of you, as if you were showing it to God. Tell him in your mind or whisper into your hands about the big request you have for him.
- *You may want to finish with a prayer* – God, we know these are big requests, but you are a big God. You are the king of kings, creator of the world, more powerful than anything else. We put these things before you and ask a big ask. We will look excitedly and patiently for your response. Thank you for listening to us, God.
- Put the object somewhere you can see, like you are leaving it out for you and God to look at it. Be patient to look for how God responds. Keep waiting and paying attention to all the different, unexpected ways God responds. Keep checking in with each other as a family about how God is responding. You may need to keep persevering in prayer as you wait for his response.

11

David
and the decision

2 Samuel 2

KEY TRUTH

God guides us.

Many of us feel paralysed or pulled in different directions when we have to make a decision. It's hard to decide what to do when uncertainty is down every path. Our children can find this particularly hard. God promises to guide us and lead us. He does this in so many different ways. In this story, we see a simple encouragement to come to God and ask for what decision we should make and be ready to say yes to his answer.

Story

David shifted uncomfortably on his bench. His knee bounced up and down with nervous energy as he watched his wife grind flour. He wanted to talk with her and get her advice, but he didn't know how to start.

'Abigail, I'm just not sure what to do!' he blurted out.

Abigail stopped and looked at him with eyebrows raised. Then she wiped her hands on her apron and smiled. 'Well, the first thing you're going to do is take over for me on this millstone while I take a break. You can work out some of those emotions while you're grinding, and I'll be able to listen to you better.'

David laughed and agreed. He loved how honest she was. It's one of the reasons he married her, and why he wanted her wisdom now.

She rocked back on her heels and stood up with a small groan. She smiled affectionately and gave him a kiss as they swapped places.

David knelt in front of the millstone, still sprinkled with grain. He placed the small upper stone on top of the grain and pressed down, and pushed and pulled the small stone forwards and back until the grain was crushed into flour and looked like sand. Abigail would use the flour to make bread later. It felt good to be doing something productive. In every other part of his life, he felt he was doing nothing.

'Okay, husband, talk to me,' said Abigail.

David sighed. Where to start? 'When I was just a teenager, God told me I'd be king one day. After all these years of pain and stress and fighting with King Saul, it's over now. He's dead. Despite all the problems I had with him, you know how sad I was when I heard he died.'

Abigail nodded.

David began to find his rhythm with the millstone. Forwards and back, forwards and back. The vibrations of the stones against each other made his arms feel slightly numb.

'Maybe now is the time for me to be king. But I'm not sure what to do next. Do I declare myself king? Do I call a meeting of the leaders of the Israelites? Can I even do that? Do I wait to see what others will do? Is being patient the right thing? Or should I be bold?' He felt crushed. 'I'm just not sure.'

David began to speed up the grinding, out of sheer frustration. He so wanted to do what was right. So many people were counting on him. One mistake could have consequences that would last a long time.

He glanced up at Abigail. She had her thinking face on.

Abigail leaned back against the wall. 'I really hate to say this now, as you're doing such a good job of grinding, but… have you asked God about it?'

David stopped grinding. Had he? No. He had made lists of ideas. He had talked to his advisors and friends. But had he simply gone to God and asked him what *he* wanted? He shook his head. 'No.'

Abigail stood up. 'God has guided you through so many tricky situations before. He told you where to fight, and how to rescue me when I got kidnapped. But he is the God who is there to guide us in big *and* small things. I suggest you ask him what small step you should do next. It's his plan that you be king. You need some guidance from him about that.'

David stared at the millstone. He slowly realised he'd been trying to figure this out all on his own. He'd been lonely doing it that way. He felt as if he were being crushed under the weight of it all, like the grain he was grinding. He only felt like that when he forgot to discuss things over with the God who loves him.

David wiped his hands and stood up. 'You're right. I need to go spend some time with God.'

He walked over to Abigail and hugged her tightly. 'Thank you,' he whispered into her hair. He could feel her smile against his chest.

'Go on, then!' she said, as she patted his back. 'Go find out what God wants you to do.' She pulled away from his hug and pushed him lightly towards the door. 'Or else I'll think you just wanted to get out of helping me!'

David jogged out of the house and towards a nearby field and then on to his favourite tree. He liked talking to God out in the fields and under trees. It felt peaceful. He could put down his work for a while, and just enjoy God.

He sat down under the shade of his favourite tree and leaned his back against the trunk and let his thoughts go.

Hi, David said to God, smiling. It was like greeting an old friend. *Here is what I'm thinking, but I want to know what you think.* David liked just thinking with God. Peace filled him as he grew aware of God listening to him.

David loved his town of Ziklag. It was home to him. But it was on the very edge of the kingdom. If God wanted him to be king, maybe it would be wise for him to move closer to God's people and get to know them better. Or maybe it didn't matter where he lived.

God, should I move back to one of the towns of Judah?

Yes, came the answer, like a small voice that he heard with his heart.

Which town should I go to, God?

To Hebron, replied the same voice that he heard with his heart.

Okay. David nodded. *We are in your mighty hands, God. I will happily obey. I love you.*

He sat under the tree for a while, chatting with God. The sun reached high in the sky, and David knew it was time to head back.

Abigail saw him coming and waved. She stood with her hands on her hips and called out to him, 'Did you and God sort out what's next?'

He smiled. 'Oh yes.'

Conversation starters

Let's answer some questions together. I'll answer them too.

- What part of the story did you like or find interesting or surprising? Why?
- What does this story tell us about God?
- It can be hard to make decisions: what school to go to, what friends' ideas to say no to or what bedroom to have in a new house. Big and small decisions happen every day. Why do you think we all sometimes forget to ask God what he thinks we should do? Or why do we choose not to ask?
- God guides us in many ways – dreams, a small quiet voice in our heart, the Bible, pictures in our mind, a feeling deep inside of what is right, or even emotions like peace or excitement. How does God help you decide what is right? Share a story of one time you felt God helped you make a decision. *(Or use a story at* **parentingforfaith.org/comfort-stories.***)*
- Abigail helped David by encouraging him to ask God. As a family we can help each other. Is there anything you think I might need to ask God about? What about you?

Connect with God

Let's connect with God and chat with him about this.

- David went outside to chat to God in his favourite place. Do you have a favourite place to chat to God? Where? Why do you like it?
- If you want to, go to one (or all) of your favourite places to chat with God. Tell God about a decision you have been struggling with and how you feel about it.
- Ask him what you should do and think with God about the situation. Don't worry about trying to make it happen. Remember sometimes God communicates with feelings, small thoughts, pictures and peace.

- *When you are done, come back to an agreed place and share what that experience was like* – What did it feel like? What was God doing? It's okay to still not be sure. The more we spend time with God, the more we will get used to catching all his communications.
- *You may want to finish with a prayer* – Thank you, God, that you promise to guide us and help us make decisions. Remind us to come and chat with you when we feel stuck or worried about decisions and help us catch what you are communicating with us.

12

No words

Genesis 16 and 21

KEY TRUTH

God can hear our prayers even when we don't know what to say.

There are times when we have so many feelings, we don't know how to talk about them. Sometimes the sadness is so big, or the uncertainty is so powerful, that we don't know what to do. God loves us so much, and knows us so well, and is with us so closely, that he can hear our hearts even without words. We can just share our emotions with God or ask him to be with us and he can understand us.

Story

Ishmael's head was throbbing. The glare of the desert sun bounced off the hot sand and hurt his eyes. He could see his mother a few steps ahead of him, shuffling along the path, leading the way as best she could.

Ishmael's mouth was dry and his throat scratchy. He was so thirsty. Their containers had run out of water days ago. And now their only hope was to find a well or a spring of water in the barren desert. 'I don't think we're going to make it,' Ishmael mumbled. 'We must be lost.'

He remembered the hug his dad gave him when they said goodbye. He could still smell his dad's thick robe and feel his rough beard against his forehead. He remembered his dad's sad voice saying, 'You'll be okay, son.'

Ishmael trudged on behind his mother. *We shouldn't even be here,* he thought. *I don't understand why Dad sent us away and said we can't live with him anymore.*

Ishmael's feet were heavy with every step. He tripped over a rock and stumbled to the ground. 'I can't keep walking, Mum,' he groaned. 'I'm just too exhausted. I need water.' He knew his body wouldn't move anymore without it. He felt defeated.

His mum brushed his cheek with her hand. 'That's okay,' she said. Her voice was weak but reassuring. 'Let's rest here. You've done so well today.' She helped him hobble over to a large bush and lie down in its shade. She kissed him on the forehead, and then whispered, 'I love you, Ishmael.'

He closed his eyes to rest, and he heard his mum stumble away. And then he thought he heard her crying.

I feel so alone, he thought. *God, are you there? God, I…*

He didn't know what to say. He had no words to express what he felt. His life was in such a jumbled mess. Sadness flowed up like a fountain inside him until he felt he was drowning in it. He began to cry loudly, and his whole body shook with emotion.

Ishmael cried for what felt like years.

Then, his attention was pulled to his mother's voice in the distance, shouting and sobbing. 'Ishmael! It's water! I have water!'

Ishmael sat up the best he could to see what was happening. He caught sight of his mother running towards him with a plump water carrier in her hands, water soaking her sleeves and dripping from her arms. Her face was beaming with joy.

'God sees us!' she called as she dropped down beside him. She scooped his head up and held the carrier to his lips. 'Drink, Ishmael. Drink.'

Ishmael sipped the water slowly. It tasted so good. And with every sip, he felt better and stronger. Ishmael looked up at his mum's radiant face and was confused. 'Where did you find this water?'

'Just over there where I was sitting,' she said, pointing to the spot. 'I heard a voice from heaven with my own ears! The angel said to me, "What is wrong, Hagar? Don't be afraid! God has heard the boy crying there. Go help the boy. Hold his hand and lead him. I will make him the father of many people." And then I looked to my left, and there was a well of water. Right next to me.' She threw her hands up and laughed and cried at the same time.

Ishmael sat quietly for a minute, just thinking about it all. 'God saved us,' he said softly.

'Yes, he did!' she said. 'Don't you see? God didn't say he heard *me*. He said he heard *you*.'

Ishmael glanced at his mum and then out towards the well. 'But, Mum, I couldn't pray. I don't think I said anything to God. I didn't know what to say. I just… cried.'

His mum gently bumped against him. 'Not all prayers have words. God didn't need words from you. He loves you. He saw you. He heard you crying. He understood what it meant. Sometimes that is prayer enough.' She smiled.

Ishmael thought about what she had said. Yes, God had *heard* his cries. God had been with him! He *wasn't* alone.

Then he remembered his old home. 'This doesn't change what happened with Dad, though,' he said, feeling a little of that sadness welling back up again.

'No, it doesn't change anything with Dad, my son. That will hurt for a while,' she sighed. 'But it does mean we have a God who has great plans for our lives.' She patted his shoulder gently. 'And we know he hears us.'

Ishmael looked out towards the well. *Thank you, God, for coming to help. I didn't have the right words, but you heard my heart anyway.*

Conversation starters

Let's answer some questions together. I'll answer them too.

- What part of the story did you like or find interesting or surprising? Why?
- What does this story tell us about God?
- Ishmael felt like his life was falling apart. He didn't know what to say to God. Have you ever felt like you didn't have the words to talk to God?
- God doesn't need words to hear what we want to express to him. He wants you to share your feelings with him, in any way you can. What are some other ways you can express yourself to God besides words?
- Share a story of a time you didn't have words to tell God how you felt, but you knew God understood you and responded to you. *(Or use a story at **parentingforfaith.org/comfort-stories**.)*

Connect with God

Let's connect with God and chat with him about this.

- God, we have so many feelings about our situation. Search us, God, and know all of our thoughts and feelings. We want you to know us.
- *Spend some time in the quiet, or listening to a song while you just rest with God, not feeling the pressure to talk to God, but just resting and inviting God to be with you.*
- *You might want to finish with a prayer* – Thank you, God, that you know us inside and out. Hear our cries and thoughts and understand all of us, even if we don't have the words yet. Thank you for loving us.

13

The risk

Acts 9 and 22

KEY TRUTH

God gives us purpose and jobs even in uncertainty.

We all feel the need to be purposeful in the world. Everyone needs to feel like they matter to others and can make a difference. When uncertainty comes into our lives, we can sometimes stand still or be so overwhelmed that we start to hold ourselves back from helping others. But God always sees us as powerful and able to help. He made us that way, and he keeps making opportunities for us to make a difference as a small part of his great plans, even in the middle of uncertainty.

Story

Ananias stood by the front door and repeated his plea: 'Mum, please stay away from the synagogue today. It's dangerous.'

His mother squeezed his arm gently. 'We can't hide every time someone wants to arrest us for knowing the truth about Jesus. We're not ashamed.' She leaned over and kissed him on the cheek and whispered, 'I'll be fine.'

Ananias' heart sank as he watched her cross the road and join her friends for a trip to the market. He worried about the dangers in Damascus these days. And now a ruthless man named Saul was coming to town to arrest *everyone* who believed in Jesus. That really scared him.

Ananias sighed and went back inside his house and closed the door. He figured he'd stay inside all day. Surely *that* would be the safest thing to do. Hide. If only he could convince his mum and her friends to do that, too!

Ananias set up a few baskets on the table and began his day's work. But he just couldn't focus. He couldn't stop thinking about being arrested. 'Oh God,' he prayed, 'keep my family safe. Keep your followers from harm. Hide us from our enemies.'

Suddenly, a voice broke through his thoughts, clear and quiet: 'Ananias!'

Ananias froze for a second. The voice didn't come from outside the house. And he wasn't even sure he heard it with his ears. But he recognised it. It was God speaking to him. His heart leaped in that moment.

The voice came again: 'Ananias!'

'Yes, Lord,' he whispered back. He put down his work and waited to hear more.

'Get up and go to the street called Straight Street. Find the house of Judas and ask for a man named Saul from the city of Tarsus. He is there now, praying. He has seen a vision in which a man named Ananias came and laid his hands on him so that he could see again.'

Fear shot through Ananias. *Saul of Tarsus? He's the man coming to arrest us! Jesus wants me to pray with him?* Ananias took a moment to calm himself. He then licked his lips together and responded carefully: 'Lord, many people have told me about this man. They told me about the many bad things he did to your holy people in Jerusalem. Now he has come here to Damascus. The leading priests have given him the power to arrest all people who trust in you.'

Jesus' firm voice returned: 'Go! I have chosen Saul for an important work. I want him to tell other nations, their rulers and the people of Israel about me. I will show him all that he must suffer for me.'

Ananias sat in silence and waited to hear more. His mind raced with questions for Jesus: *Will I be safe if I go? What should I say to Saul?* But there was only silence.

Ananias glanced at the closed door. 'Okay,' he said aloud, trying to make sense of it all. 'I can either stay home and feel safe or go and pray for Saul, even if I'm scared.'

Ananias took a few deep breaths, and his heart started beating faster as he made his decision: 'Lord, I'm scared, but I'll do everything you've told me to do. I *really* want to be a part of your plan.'

Ananias took one last deep breath and swung around to pick up his cloak, and then he dashed out the door. He prayed as he hurried through the streets until he found the house of Judas in Straight Street. The house was there, all right, just as Jesus said. Gulping once, Ananias knocked… and waited.

'Who is it?' came a voice from behind the door.

'I'm Ananias. I was told to come here.'

The door unlocked with a loud clank and then swung open. A smiling man greeted him. 'I'm Judas,' he said. 'Come in. Come in! We've been waiting for you!'

Ananias followed him into the main room where a small man lay on a bed against the wall.

Judas stooped down and softly shook the man's arm. 'Saul, Saul, Ananias has come to see you, just as the Lord said he would!' Judas carefully helped him sit up.

'So where is this man called Ananias?' asked Saul. He stared straight ahead, as if waiting for something.

'I'm here, Saul,' said Ananias, stepping closer. He could see that Saul's eyes were grey and cloudy. He was definitely blind. Ananias stood there and just looked at him for a second. *Is this the Saul who was going to arrest us all and throw us in prison?* he wondered. *He looks so helpless and confused!*

Ananias' fear slowly began to melt away. And in its place, God's love began to well up inside him. Ananias then understood: Saul simply needed Jesus, like everyone else.

Ananias touched Saul's shoulders. 'Saul, my brother, the Lord Jesus sent me.' Saul nodded as Ananias continued: 'He is the one you saw on the road when you came here. He sent me so that you can see again and also be filled with the Holy Spirit.' Then tears began to trickle down Ananias' face. 'Saul, my brother, look up and see again!'

In that instant, Saul began to breathe deeply and peacefully as the Holy Spirit touched him, and then something like scales fell from his eyes. Soon Saul's face erupted in joy. 'I can see! I can see!' he burst out. He blinked several times, trying to adjust his eyes to the light, and then he smiled in amazement and said, 'Jesus really *is* who he says he is!'

'Yes! Yes, he is!' said Judas. He laughed with happiness.

Ananias sat back and grinned at Judas and Saul as they laughed and celebrated what God had just done. Then he sighed. *I almost let my fear keep me at home today. I could have missed this whole thing. I'm so glad I didn't.*

Conversation starters

Let's answer some questions together. I'll answer them too.

- What part of the story did you like or find interesting or surprising? Why?
- What does this story tell us about God?
- Ananias was afraid. He wanted to stay at home and be safe, until God asked him to do something. But that didn't make him feel more brave, only more scared! Have you ever felt that God might be asking you to do something and you were scared to do it? *(Or use a story at **parentingforfaith.org/comfort-stories**.)*
- Why would God give Ananias a job when he knew Ananias was scared and wanting to hide?
- Ananias' fear went away when he met Saul, because he saw that God loved Saul and that Saul needed God. God's love was stronger than Ananias' fear. How can we focus on God's love when we are afraid?

Connect with God

Let's connect with God and chat with him about this.

- Tell God in your head or whisper into your hands how you are feeling about helping others. If 1 is 'I want to hide from everybody' and 10 is 'I'm ready to help always', what number are you on that scale?
- Tell God what scares you about saying yes to God's jobs.
- Tell God what you would need help with if you were to say yes to God's jobs.
- *You might want to finish with a prayer* – God, we are all different and experience different levels of feeling afraid or wanting to hide. Please fill us with your love, so we can know how much you love us. Please fill us with your love for others so we can see them like you do. Some of us want to say, 'Here I am God, send me.' (If you

want to tell God that, feel free to do so in your head or whisper it into your hands.) Thank you that you love us and even in the middle of our difficult circumstances, you want us to be powerful ministers of your kingdom.

14

The short way home

Luke 15:11-31

When people go through uncertainty, we sometimes can make mistakes and poor choices. We can sometimes feel guilt and shame that can weigh us down and make us feel disconnected from God. One of the greatest uncertainties in life is when we are unsure whether God still loves us because of the bad things we've thought or done. But we do not need to worry, because God is ready and waiting for us to run to him, no matter what we've done.

Story

Ben's knees hurt. He had been picking up little brown pods from under the carob tree for hours, and his whole body ached. He straightened up and tried to stretch his back.

'Ben!' whispered Javad, the worker at the next tree over.

'What?' Ben replied.

Javad looked around. 'I'm going to eat some of these carob pods. I'm starving.'

Ben quickly glanced at the overseer. The man was pacing back and forth, eyeing every move the workers made. 'Don't do it, Javad,' Ben whispered. 'You know we'll get in trouble. These pods are for the master's pigs to eat, not us. Last week they fired a guy for eating one. Don't you remember? They beat him up and kicked him out.'

Javad grunted in frustration. 'Fine. Then distract me. Talk to me. Tell me the story of how you ended up working here.'

Ben rolled his eyes. 'I don't know,' he said, reluctantly.

Javad threw a carob pod at him. 'Come on, man! The way you talk tells me that you were posh once. How did you end up picking food for pigs? It's got to be a good enough story to take my mind off my stomach!'

Ben sighed. That was the last story he wanted to tell. He could feel his face getting red just thinking about it. It was easier to pretend it just never happened.

Ben scooped up some pods and put them in the basket and shuffled forward to a new pile. 'I wasn't posh, but my dad did have quite a lot of money. He had people working for him in our house and on our farms and fields. People like you and me now, I guess.'

The overseer walked past. Ben and Javad sped up their gathering to look as if they were working hard.

Ben hated that overseer. He was cruel and unfair. He never really gave them enough to eat so they were always hungry.

Ben didn't want Javad to think his dad was cruel like that. 'My dad always treated the workers in our fields really well. He paid them fairly, and he made sure they always had plenty to eat. They were like part of the family. My dad is a really good man.'

Javad looked confused. 'So why are you in a totally different country slowly starving to death?'

Ben got quiet. 'I'm here because I made some really bad choices.' Something like a sob tried to get out of Ben, but he pushed it back down. He didn't want to cry. If he started, he might not be able to stop.

'I wanted to get out and live my own life. So I asked Dad to give me the money he had saved for me, and I left.' Ben's voice cracked and he took a deep breath. Just remembering that conversation with his father overwhelmed him.

'I said some really awful, hurtful things. I will always remember how crushed my dad looked. But I didn't care. I just wanted my money.'

Ben was so ashamed he had hurt his father. He would do anything to change the past, but there was nothing he could do.

The overseer glared at them as they emptied their baskets into the cart and continued to the next tree. Javad patted Ben's shoulder. 'I'm so sorry, mate. I didn't know.'

Ben nodded and knelt back down on to his sore knees. 'The rest of the story is fairly straightforward. I took the money and came to this country. I spent all my money on stupid things. Fancy clothes and houses and treating my friends to nice things. I spent it all.'

Sweat dripped down Ben's neck as he lifted another armful of pods into the basket. 'I had no food, no place to live, no money and no family. So I begged for a job at this place.' Ben waved his arm at the grove of trees around him. 'The worst place to work ever.'

Javad laughed under his breath and glanced at the overseer. 'It is really bad here. But to be fair, I didn't know farms like your dad's existed. Plenty of food and getting paid fair wages? Unheard of!'

Ben weakly smiled and leaned forward to scoop up more pods. He did remember how happy his dad's workers were. After having worked here, his dad's farm sounded like paradise.

Ben's mind began to churn an idea. He would never be accepted back home as a son. He had hurt his dad and wasted his money. He wasn't good enough to be his dad's son anymore. But his dad was a good boss. Maybe, just maybe, if he apologised to his dad, his dad would hire him to be a worker in *his* fields. At least he wouldn't be starving anymore. And maybe he would once in a while, from far away, get to see his dad smile.

Ben decided to do it. He stood up and brushed his knees. 'Javad, I'm going back. I'm going to beg my dad to hire me as a worker because I can't go back as his son.' Ben smiled at Javad. 'I'll send you directions later.' He turned to the approaching overseer and said forcefully, 'I quit!'

After many months of travelling, the road in front of Ben became more and more familiar. The air began to smell like home, warm and thick with lavender bushes and acacia trees. The vibrant green of the fields made him smile, and he began to feel more like himself with every step of the way.

But the closer Ben got to his home, the greater he felt the weight of his shame. His mind filled with doubts. What if his dad refused to see him? What if his dad threw him out, not even letting him work in the fields because he hated him so much? What if his mistakes were too big to forgive? He kicked a rock on the dusty path. If the worst happened, he deserved it.

Ben paused on the road. Far off in the distance he could see the smoke rising from the chimney of his family home. His heart started racing and he felt sick. He practised his speech one more time under his breath: 'Father, I have sinned against God and done wrong to you. I am so sorry. I know I am not worthy to be called your son. But please may I come and be a worker in your field?'

It wouldn't be enough. There weren't enough words to say how much regret he had.

Ben caught sight of some movement near the door of the house. He took a few steps forward and squinted to see what it was. It appeared to be someone running. Towards him.

'Ben!' His father's voice broke through the air. 'Ben!'

Ben searched his father's face for signs of anger. Instead, he saw a huge smile.

Within seconds, his father had closed the gap between them and pulled Ben towards him into a powerful hug. 'You are home! You are home!' His father showered his head with kisses.

All the emotion of the past months erupted out of Ben. He began to sob. He tried to get the words out, 'I'm so sorry, Dad. I'm so sorry,' while his dad held him tightly.

After what seemed like hours, his dad pulled back a little to wipe the tears off Ben's cheek, and he finally looked at him, face to face.

His dad's face was full of love, and Ben could see his dad had been crying too. Ben couldn't bear it anymore. 'I'm so sorry, Dad. I sinned against God and was so awful to you. I know that I'm not worthy to be your son.' His tears began to flow again. 'But maybe I can work in your fields.'

His dad wrapped his arms around his son again as Ben buried his face in his dad's chest. He heard his dad's muffled voice saying, 'I love you, Ben. I am so happy you are home.'

After a while, his dad took a big breath and stepped back, still holding Ben's arms. 'Right,' he said. 'Let's have a welcome home party.'

His dad spun around and started yelling for people to come and sort out clothes and food for a huge welcome home feast.

Ben followed slowly, finally empty of tears. He felt a peace that he never expected to feel again. He was forgiven and welcomed back. Ben took a deep, shaky breath and smiled.

His shame was completely gone. The love of his father had washed it all away.

Conversation starters

Let's answer some questions together. I'll answer them too.

- What part of the story did you like or find interesting or surprising? Why?
- What does this story tell us about God?
- Shame is the feeling we have when we know the choices or mistakes we made were not right, and we are embarrassed, sad or disappointed that we did those things. It can make us want to stay away from God and sometimes from other people we have hurt. Have you ever felt that feeling? How did you feel about yourself? How did you feel about talking to the people you hurt or about God?
- God doesn't want us to run away from him when we make mistakes or bad choices (called 'sin'). He wants us to come to him, like the son in the story. What does it feel like when you run to God and feel his love and forgiveness? *(Or use a story at **parentingforfaith.org/comfort-stories**.)*

Connect with God

Let's connect with God and chat with him about this.

- Whenever we feel shame, or know we've done something wrong, we can run to God about it. We can try it out now.
- Think of something that you maybe know you did wrong and you haven't talked to God about it yet.
- Tell God about it either in your head or by whispering in your hand. Tell him the story and how it made you feel. *(Pause to give time for the conversation.)*
- However you want to, ask God for forgiveness. Some people say, 'I want to change' or 'I'm sorry I did that' or even simply 'Will you forgive me?' There are no right words to say, just tell God what you want.
- Let's wait in the quiet as God comes close and lets us feel his love. Feel free to chat to him or just sit peacefully.
- *You may want to finish with a prayer* – Thank you, God, that you wipe away our sins because of what Jesus did on the cross for us. Thank you for loving us and forgiving us, so we can live close to you. We love you, God.

15

Until we meet again

Acts 6-7 and 20-21

KEY TRUTH
Because of Jesus, death is not goodbye.

When Jesus died on the cross and came back to life, he made a way for us to live with God forever. Death is not the end. We have more life after death, forever with God and all others who have followed Jesus. While we deeply miss those we love when they die, we can be confident that death is not goodbye forever for those who love God.

Story

The strong sea wind whipped Philip's hair as he smiled at the busy harbour. Rows of ships jostled side by side on the glistening green-blue water. He loved how huge merchant ships bringing spices and cloth from across the world bumped gently alongside the small local fishing boats. While the big ships were beautiful, it was the fishing boats that had his heart.

A whiff of the marketplace food stalls drifted over to him, and his stomach rumbled. He sent his friends Paul and Luke to the food stalls a while ago, and they seemed to be taking a long time. He turned to look and saw them walking towards him with eager smiles and hands full of steaming hot fish wrapped in flatbread.

'I love it here!' Luke said as he handed Philip his food.

Philip laughed. 'Well, I'm glad you stopped by here on your journeys. People need to hear about Jesus, and anything we can do to help you spread the word, we will do!'

Paul took a huge bite of his food and made a little satisfied noise. Philip grinned and told Luke, 'I've known Paul for a very long time. I can rarely find food he enjoys that much.'

Paul laughed and chewed. 'You've bragged about this famous Caesarea food, and I can finally say for once you were right.' The three erupted in laughter.

'Where are you headed next, do you think?' Philip asked.

'Back to Jerusalem.' Paul said as he took another bite.

Philip paused. 'Jerusalem? Hasn't there been quite a lot of trouble for followers of Jesus in Jerusalem recently.'

Paul nodded with a little shrug. 'It's hard everywhere.'

Philip smiled. If anyone knew how to handle rough crowds, it was Paul.

'Paul! Paul! Look who it is!' Luke pointed across the harbour to an older man heading towards them with determination. His long grey hair floated behind him like a flag in the wind. He walked slightly hunched over, and his knees poked the sides of his robe as he stomped towards them.

'Agabus!' Paul smiled at the new arrival. 'How are you? What are you doing here?'

Agabus' eyebrows were furrowed. 'I came with a message from the Holy Spirit,' he said.

Paul handed his food to Luke and wiped his hands clean. 'I'm ready to hear.'

Agabus reached out to Paul and awkwardly began to untie the thin rope that was wrapped around Paul's waist like a belt.

Paul watched and waited patiently as the old man's gnarled hands struggled with the knot, until the belt finally came off.

Then Agabus sat down on the stone path and began to wrap the thin rope around his own hands and ankles, until he was sat completely bound, unable to move.

Agabus said in a quiet voice, 'The Holy Spirit tells me, "This is how the Jews in Jerusalem will tie up the man who wears this belt. Then they will hand him over to people who don't know God."'

A flash of fear gripped Philip's heart. Paul wasn't just going to Jerusalem to preach about Jesus. Paul was going to be arrested, tied up and handed to the Romans.

As he knelt to help Agabus get untied, Philip spoke softly to Paul, 'You can't go to Jerusalem now. You heard what the Holy Spirit said through Agabus. It's not safe. They will arrest you. I'm afraid they will do worse. Like they did to Stephen. They killed him.'

Paul sat on the low wall of the harbour. 'I know it's dangerous. But, for quite some time, the Holy Spirit has been clear to me that prison and hardships are in my future. I don't know exactly what will happen in Jerusalem. I just know I'm supposed to go. I am willing to be put in jail in Jerusalem. I am even ready to die for the name of the Lord Jesus!'

A well of worry opened up within Philip. He knew he couldn't talk Paul out of going, not once Paul felt that God was sending him. He couldn't protect his friend. He might lose him.

Luke jumped in to encourage Paul. 'God has rescued you and our friends so many times from disaster. Maybe we'll see another miracle to get you out of prison!'

Paul turned to Luke. 'All I want is to be faithful to do what God told me to do. And when it's time for me to die, I want to die like Stephen did.'

Philip felt sick. 'You want to be stoned to death in front of an angry mob?' Hot tears began to burn in Philip's eyes. He didn't want that path for Paul. He didn't want Paul to suffer or be hurt. He didn't want him to die.

'No,' Paul said. His eyes were gentle as he looked at Philip. 'I was there when your friend was killed. Do you remember the look on his face right before he died?'

Philip searched his memory. Stephen's face. He did remember. In the moment before he died, Stephen's face glowed with joy and peace.

Paul continued quietly, 'Do you remember him calling out to all of us, "Look! I see heaven open. And I see the Son of Man standing at God's right side. Lord Jesus, receive my spirit!" Right before he died, Stephen wasn't seeing a crowd of angry people. He was seeing Jesus with his own eyes! He looked so full of love and confidence. He knew exactly where he was going when he died and who was waiting for him.'

Philip felt peace begin to rise like a flood within him. This was the truth.

Paul smiled. 'Death doesn't scare me. When I die, Jesus will still be waiting for me at the right hand of God with Stephen and James and so many of our friends and family. There is only hope here. Whatever happens in Jerusalem, prison or death, I belong to Jesus and will go where he tells me to go.'

Philip wrapped Paul in a hug. 'I agree. Whatever comes in Jerusalem, we will be praying for you. That you will know the closeness of God, and always have that hope and surety of where Jesus sends you.'

Philip let go of Paul and stepped back with a teary smile. 'Well, then,' Philip said, 'whatever happens, this is not goodbye. However it turns out, I will see you again. On earth or in heaven.'

Paul nodded emphatically. 'Count on it.'

Conversation starters

Let's answer some questions together. I'll answer them too.

- What part of the story did you like or find interesting or surprising? Why?
- What does this story tell us about God?
- Why wasn't Paul scared of dying?
- Do you know anyone who has died? How do you feel when you think about them?

Connect with God

Let's connect with God and chat with him about this.

- When Jesus was on earth, one of his friends died. He sat with his friend's sisters and cried. Even though he knew he would see his friend again, he still cried. It's okay to feel sad and still know you will see your loved one again. Jesus died on the cross and came back to life so that death doesn't have to be goodbye, but so we can spend forever together. But that doesn't mean we don't have lots of emotions here, now. Tell God in your head or whisper into your hand what you loved about *(name the person who died)*. Tell God all about them. Ask God what he loves about them too. Draw a picture or write it out if you like. *(Take as much time as you need.)*
- Tell God how you feel about missing your loved one.
- Ask God to fill you with his love and comfort. *(Wait in silence, and breathe as God comes close.)*
- *You may want to finish with a prayer* – God, we miss *(name the person)* so much, and our hearts feel torn sometimes. Thank you, Jesus, for coming and dying on the cross and rising again so that one day we may all be together with you. We are so looking forward to one day laughing and playing together again. Until then, please hug us close. Remind us of all the wonderful memories we have, and help us when we need your love and comfort.

About Parenting for Faith

It's tempting for families to leave the 'faith stuff' to church… yet it's so much more powerful when parents help children and teens see everyday life through the eyes of faith.

Parenting for Faith is a ministry of BRF, pioneered by Rachel Turner, an experienced children's, youth and family pastor. Our vision is to give you, as a parent, grandparent or caregiver, the confidence and skills to foster your child's relationship with God, so it becomes real, personal, lasting and rooted in the everyday ups and downs of family life.

That means helping you become confident role models as you demonstrate a life of faith. It's about enabling you to recognise and share where God might be, in the hurly burly of your family's week. We won't give you formulas to follow: we'll help you develop ways that feel natural within your own family and church culture, for you and your children to talk to God and hear from him… to respond to him and to celebrate him!

We aim to offer encouragement, nurturing and training – not just for parents, grandparents and caregivers, but also for the church leaders who support them. Here's what some people have said about Parenting for Faith:

> 'Rachel's enthusiasm is infectious. She brings a depth of knowledge and experience which we have all found encouraging. We have learned much about how to engage with the faith of our children and to raise "God-connected" kids.'

> 'I love that the teaching is so practical and useful.'

Find out more at **parentingforfaith.org**

Stay connected!

Do you hope to raise children and teens who stay connected to God throughout their life's journey? The good news is you can! We believe God has placed you in the perfect position to do just that. We'd love you to be part of our supportive community of parents, extended family members, carers and church leaders, so you can find exactly the help and encouragement you're looking for, 24/7.

Find us on social media

 facebook.com/parentingforfaithBRF

 twitter.com/godconnected

 instagram.com/parentingforfaithbrf

▶ YouTube youtube.com/brfcharity

The Parenting for Faith podcast

Don't miss our regular Parenting for Faith podcast covering up-to-the-minute issues, questions from parents like you, special guests and interviews. Find it wherever you normally listen to podcasts or go to **parentingforfaith.org/podcast**.

Reflections and suggestions online

Maybe you're wondering how to help your kids cope with challenges at school or what to do about Halloween. Perhaps your children feel God can't love them because of what they're going through or you're trying to help them develop gratitude. You might be struggling to know how to help a child with additional needs connect with God.

Whatever your concern, you can be sure someone has been there before you. We've commissioned a collection of well over 300 topics, from the Parenting for Faith team and from parents just like you, writing and speaking from their own experience.

Find just what you need, just when you need it, in the searchable library at **parentingforfaith.org/topics**.

The Parenting for Faith course

> *Doing the course was life-changing in terms of my parenting, and it was amazing as a pastor to see significant changes happening in the lives of the participants. We can't wait to run it again!*
> Course participant

If you're looking to transform how you do faith in the home, why not think about running our video-based course in your church, among your friends or even by yourself or with a family member? People regularly tell us it's been a 'game changer', bringing renewal not just to families but to whole churches.

The Parenting for Faith course is available to download or live-stream from any device, with free handbooks and promotional materials for groups. For those who prefer DVDs and printed handbooks, these are available to buy from BRF.

Find out more at **parentingforfaith.org/course**.

Enabling all ages to grow in faith

Anna Chaplaincy

Living Faith

Messy Church

Parenting for Faith

100 years of BRF

2022 is BRF's 100th anniversary! Look out for details of our special new centenary resources, a beautiful centenary rose and an online thanksgiving service that we hope you'll attend. This centenary year we're focusing on sharing the story of BRF, the story of the Bible – and we hope you'll share your stories of faith with us too.

Find out more at **brf.org.uk/centenary**.

To find out more about our work, visit

brf.org.uk